A MULTIFAITH GUIDE TO CREATING PERSONAL PRAYER IN YOUR LIFE

SECRETS *of* PRAYER

NANCY CORCORAN, CSJ

Walking Together, Finding the Way®
SKYLIGHT PATHS®
PUBLISHING
Woodstock, Vermont

Secrets of Prayer:
A Multifaith Guide to Creating Personal Prayer in Your Life

Library of Congress Cataloging-in-Publication Data
Corcoran, Nancy.
Secrets of prayer : a multifaith guide to creating personal prayer in your life / Nancy Corcoran.
     p. cm.
Includes bibliographical references.
ISBN-13: 978-1-59473-215-7 (quality pbk.)
ISBN-10: 1-59473-215-9 (quality pbk.)
1. Prayer. 2. Spiritual life. I. Title.

BL560.C655 2007
204'.3—dc22
                                                                    2007013431

10   9   8   7   6   5   4   3   2   1

Manufactured in the United States of America

Cover Design: Jenny Buono

SkyLight Paths Publishing is creating a place where people of different spiritual traditions come together for challenge and inspiration, a place where we can help each other understand the mystery that lies at the heart of our existence.

SkyLight Paths sees both believers and seekers as a community that increasingly transcends traditional boundaries of religion and denomination—people wanting to learn from each other, *walking together, finding the way.*®

SkyLight Paths, "Walking Together, Finding the Way" and colophon are trademarks of LongHill Partners, Inc., registered in the U.S. Patent and Trademark Office.

Walking Together, Finding the Way®
Published by SkyLight Paths Publishing
A Division of LongHill Partners, Inc.
Sunset Farm Offices, Route 4, P.O. Box 237
Woodstock, VT 05091
Tel: (802) 457-4000   Fax: (802) 457-4004
www.skylightpaths.com

To my Carondelet community
    for sharing such a rich life with me
Especially Abbott to Zilch
    and all those in between

Mary Elizabeth,
may you remember Jesus's words —
"Love your neighbor as
    yourself"
you first!!!
    It's a god thing!
        Nancy
        Corcoran

Where is that secret place—dost thou ask, "Where?"
O soul, it is the secret place of prayer!

—*Alfred Lord Tennyson*

CONTENTS

INTRODUCTION

I have lived with serious pray-ers for most of my life: For thirty-five years I have been a Catholic sister. Some may think that gives me extra credibility or inside knowledge in the prayer lineup, but even among these wonderful women, I don't know any one of us who thinks she prays well. (It's interesting to note that, when I entered the convent, prayer ranked *second* in top values for sisters/nuns. Cleanliness—read "housecleaning"—ranked first! Folks who know me have always wondered how I ever made it … I almost didn't! But that is for another book.)

Many people have a stereotype of a sister/nun as someone who prays all the time. Well, let me break that stereotype: We don't … and yet we do. It depends on what you mean by "prayer"—which is one of the reasons I'm writing this book. I don't know any sister/nun who thinks she has prayer down pat or knows all there is to know about prayer. My experience is that we are all learners, struggling to pray. So with that understanding, if you are one of us who is not sure what prayer is, how to pray, or why you pray, read on!

I have spent most of my adult life seeking the meaning in prayer, and in my search, I've discovered some secrets about prayer. I'm not talking about the kind of secrets that only a few privileged can know, but rather something more along the lines of something that is right there in front of us, but we miss it if we don't know how to look for it. I think prayer is like air: It's there all the time, but we don't have the ways to see it. We may think, "That can't be prayer!" Or we may have been taught that our religious tradition has the *only* truth about prayer, and we miss the secrets that are "hidden" to us in other faith traditions. We may not even be aware of the many possible ways of expressing our yearnings for God.

Here's the first thing I discovered in my search: Only when we begin to understand that no one has an exclusive inside track on the secrets of prayer can we truly begin to deepen our quest for the Holy.

I was slow to come to this realization, being a cradle Roman Catholic raised with an Irish ghetto mentality in provincial Boston. I was taught to believe that there was no salvation outside the Catholic Church, that Joseph McCarthy was a good guy trying to get the Commies, and that the Vietnam War was a just war. Then came the sixties and Vatican II. Pope John XXIII called on the Roman Catholic Church to renew itself, and he launched a three-year meeting of all the bishops (and a few female observers). The results? The Roman Catholic Church abandoned the universal Latin liturgy, acknowledged ecumenism, encouraged experimentation, and called for the reformation of religious life. During my senior year at college, I went from being condemned to hell for eating meat on Friday to voluntarily fasting during Advent and Lent; from attending Mass said in Latin to Mass in the vernacular (that is, English) with guitars. I could even go to a non-Catholic church without fear of "losing my faith." During the same period, the civil rights movement and the second wave of feminist thought crept into my consciousness as it exploded across the nation. The first cracks in my cosmic egg were definitely noticeable.

Then when I was twenty-one, I went from the Boston Catholic ghetto in which I was raised to Waipahu, Hawaii, where I became acquainted with Asian cultures, Buddhism, and the ancient Hawaiian religion. I was a universe away from my roots, and I began to question my fixed cultural concepts at every turn. The cracks in my cosmic egg were spreading rapidly.

Later, I journeyed to Japan, Egypt, Kenya, and Nigeria, where I met people who followed indigenous belief systems, people who were Buddhist or Shinto, and people without any religious practice. My worldview exploded. When I returned to the States, living in African American communities in Missouri, Alabama, and Mississippi stretched me further in amazing ways.

I had gone from believing in "the one true church," from believing that I had all the truth I would ever need, to becoming a student of the Holy in all forms. I had begun to understand, like Celie in *The Color Purple*, that the Creator of the cosmos was ever so much bigger than the old white man in the sky, and I wanted to find out more about the ways in which women and men of differing cultures and traditions expressed the sacred in their lives.

From there, my informal study and work with varieties of cultures led to more formal study in Asian cultures, African American cultures, and Mexican American cultures, ethics from a Jewish perspective, and Islamic history. I took theology classes at the Black Catholic Institute, did course work with Huston Smith at Boston College, took more theology courses at St. Louis University Divinity School, and ultimately entered a graduate program at Harvard Divinity School that led to a master's degree in theological studies. Reading and studying and learning from Buddhists, Muslims, Jews, and a variety of Christian denominations fully and finally cracked my cosmic egg wide open.

If I had to summarize the key that unlocked the secrets of prayer, it would be this: *No one has a corner on the Divine; no one holds all* *the secrets.* As I explored a wide diversity of beliefs and religious traditions, my concept of the Holy broke out of the small box in which I had carefully guarded it, and I felt liberated. I began adopting prayer practices that I found useful, and my prayer life became much the richer. I discovered faith traditions that don't limit themselves to expressing connections to God in words, but rather use art forms—sculpture, painting, fiber art, and more—to be in God's presence. I encountered others who called God by a variety of names: G-D, God, G*D, YHWH, Jehovah, Lord, Allah, Godde, the Holy, the Divine, the One, the Source, Spirit, the Alpha and Omega, and the Cause. And I gained a new respect for the many forms of wordless prayer, from meditation and contemplation to movement and gestures.

Perhaps the most important thing I learned is that the Holy is so much greater than what any one teaching could ever tell us, what any one person can know. Ultimately, it is up to each of us to find the spiritual practices that feed our spirits and connect us with the sacred. Even though my approach to prayer has become more universal, my practice has become more particular, more *mine*. And I have developed a steadfast belief that we each have a responsibility to seek the Divine for ourselves, to trust our own journey.

Secrets of Prayer will take you beyond any one tradition to explore and make room for the "more," the unseen, the hoped-for in your own prayer. Starting with the three most common ways faith traditions teach us to reach out to God—prayer, meditation, and contemplation—we'll move into other methods of listening for the Divine, ways of being aware of and existing in God's presence. You'll find ways to tap into the hidden sources of energy within your body to fuel your prayer and discover ways in which prayer mirrors your human needs for nourishment. Samplings of prayers from other traditions and faiths, along with stories, will help you listen to and be with the One-you-seek-who-seeks-you and broaden your approach to the vehicle of prayer. At each step along the way, practical prayer exercises offer you a chance to explore a variety of prayer practices to find what best suits you.

Whether you struggle with even the *concept* of communicating with the Holy, or you want to develop a prayer practice but are not sure where to begin, or you wish to deepen your practice, read on. *Secrets of Prayer* offers creative approaches to the Divine that may affirm what you are already doing—or help you discover that you are already practicing something you did not think to call prayer! As your understanding of the richness found in other traditions grows, you will not only feel more secure in your prayer practices, but you will also encounter some novel ways to approach the sacred.

There are many ways to climb a mountain. Some get a four-wheeler and drive right up over boulders. Others are into hiking and enjoy the gradual movement up, camping at different spots along the way. The truly daring grab their gear and climb straight up walls of rock and ice. A very few are dropped off by helicopters and are only interested in skiing down. Then, of course, there are those of us who are content to stay below and gaze up at the beauty of the mountain against the blue sky. Whatever feeds your soul, the sacred is there waiting for you. All you need to do is approach.

Secret 1

There Are Multiple Ways of Experiencing the Holy

> We may think of prayer as thoughts or feelings expressed in words, but this is only one expression. Deep prayer is the laying aside of thoughts. It is the opening of mind and heart, body and feelings—our whole being—to God, the Ultimate Mystery, beyond words, thoughts and emotions.
>
> —*Thomas Keating*

When my grandnieces first began to speak, they were very frustrated in their attempts to communicate. Garbled sounds flowed from their lips as they attempted to form the words they had been hearing for months. We tried our best to figure out what they needed or wanted, but the truth was, we really didn't care that they could not speak their words clearly. We loved that they were trying to communicate with us. We rejoiced when our attempts at understanding their communication were successful. As the months wore on, they became very proficient, and today they have no difficulty speaking with us.

Oh, their vocabulary is still limited. Elizabeth wants to be a "vegetarian" when she grows up so she can take care of sick animals. Abigail pesters us to know the meaning of the words we spell. Knowing the right words to say is more important to them than it is to us. We listen attentively and love them, even though they are not speaking perfectly.

I am reminded of the words of the master, Jesus: "If you, with all your faults, know how to give your children good things, how much more will our heavenly Abba give the Holy Spirit to those who ask?" (Matthew 7:11, *The Inclusive New Testament*).

Those who ask. Some would say that is a basic definition of people who pray. After all, we derive the English word *prayer* from the Latin word *precarius,* meaning something obtained by begging.

Yet many are intimidated by the thought of even approaching the Holy, let alone asking for something directly. Is it because we have been taught that we are unworthy to approach the Holy? Or do we believe that there are only *right* ways to pray, that we could not possibly pray properly? Or do we feel that we are not as good as we might be and fear that there is no way the Divine will respond to our feeble requests?

Fortunately, although our traditions influence our perspective, the Divine that we seek is not limited by our small boxes of perception or understanding. The secrets of prayer are there for everyone who is seeking. But to find these secrets, we have to go beyond what we know to a position of seeking and openness.

If we were to survey the world's major religions, we would find three common practices that people use as ways of reaching to God: *prayer* (communicating with the Holy), *meditation* (listening to the Holy), and *contemplation* (being with the Holy). Though these terms are often used interchangeably, they are distinct practices. That said, paradoxically they are one because they are all ways of, to use Trappist monk Thomas Keating's words, "opening our whole being to the Ultimate Mystery."

I like to use the metaphor of pregnancy, labor, and birth as a way of understanding the distinction—and connection—among these prayer practices. A woman who knows she is pregnant often begins to communicate with the life form that is developing within her (prayer). During the pregnancy, she often disciplines herself in preparation for the birth by focusing her breathing, concentrating, moving into single-mindedness (meditation). When giving birth, she must use all her knowledge in the midst of great pain. Then she sees the baby ... and ahhh, the awe is overwhelming ... words meaningless ... joy abundant! She contemplates the miracle (contemplation).

Another way to think of the differences among prayer, meditation, and contemplation is to think of them as *exoteric* and *esoteric*. *Exoteric* is that which is presented to the public. It is information that is easily accessible, popular knowledge that is comprehensible to most people. What we typically call prayer most often falls into this area because teachings about prayer in each of our religious traditions are widespread and easily accessible to the general public.

Meditation and contemplation, however, belong more to the *esoteric*. *Esoteric* refers to knowledge that is understood only by those specially initiated, teachings that are restricted to a small group, or information shared with a restricted number of people. For example, among Hindus, these people would be yogis; among Buddhists, they would be Zen masters, or Roshi; in Judaism, they would be teachers of the Kabbalah. Christians would call them mystics; Muslims might refer to them as Sufis.

Since the practice of what we traditionally call prayer is the most common form of addressing the Holy and is found almost universally across religious boundaries, it is a good place to start our exploration.

Communicating with the Holy

Prayer is a cry of hope.
—*French proverb*

What is prayer and why do we pray?

In every religious tradition, prayer is hope. Hope that we are not alone, hope that there is meaning to life. We hope because we do not know for sure.

Hope lets us believe that there is more than the physical reality we can perceive. When I became a woman of a certain age, I realized in a whole new way that the end is in sight. A friend of mine corrected me and suggested that "The end is *insight*"! I find this a much more hopeful way of perceiving the life process—and of approaching the Holy One.

Prayer is asking, seeking, praising, blessing, thanking, singing, moaning, yelling, arguing, pleading, interceding, worshiping, moving, reading, studying, being present, and being silent. Prayer is written, spontaneous, rote, memorized, repetitious, awkward, intimate, tentative, and certain. Prayer is intentional. Sometimes, prayer is unplanned. (Anyone who has driven with me knows that when I am cut off by another driver, holy words fly off my tongue. I wonder whether this is prayer.)

Prayer fluctuates. Prayers are not always hopeful, not always conscious. I don't know anyone who thinks that he or she prays well. It's not like a marathon. Being first or the fastest doesn't make a difference. My friend Jean, who is a convert to Christianity, says of herself when speaking of prayer, "I'm a flop. I can't say words as pretty as the way they appear in the King James Version, so I just read. That's my prayer."

Prayer has been a reality in my life since I was five years old and my aunt Catherine took me under her wing, listening to my early recitations of prayers and becoming my private tutor as I prepared for my first confession and Holy Communion. One of the most prayer-filled experiences of my growing-up years happened while walking alone to high school during my freshman year. As I climbed the hill near my house, I passed a Unitarian church (which I was forbidden to enter!) that had an enclosed bulletin board outside. Each week a different one-sentence sermon would appear: "If there is no struggle, there is no progress" (Frederick Douglass); "There are two ways of spreading light: to be the candle or the mirror which reflects it" (Edith Wharton); "Religious ends are in need of our deeds" (Abraham Joshua Heschel).

This was the first time I understood that prayer could be done anywhere and anytime. I could see the sign the entire time I was walking up the hill, and I would think about the quotation and ponder what it might mean. That nine months of walking reflection was my first experience of "praying in the ordinary."

Perhaps you have heard the story of the young priest who asked his pastor whether he could smoke while he prayed. The pastor responded, "Of course not." Later the priest asked whether he could pray while he smoked, and the pastor responded, "Of course! You can pray anytime." Perspective is everything.

I love the way this story of the taxi driver and the priest, who both died and went to heaven on the same day, humorously illustrates "perspective":

As they stood in line waiting for St. Peter to let them in, they began talking. When they reached St. Peter, he asked the taxi driver his name and occupation.

"Ahhh, yes," said Peter, "I have you right here." And he proceeded to garb the taxi driver with a beautiful robe and many jewels. "Enter the Kingdom of Heaven!"

St. Peter then turned to the priest. Again, Peter asked the man his name and occupation. Then Peter gave the priest a simple garment with no jewels. The priest was puzzled. He asked Peter why the taxi driver received such a glorious garment while he did not.

"Ahhh," said Peter, "up here we are only interested in results. When you preached, they slept! When he drove, they prayed!"

Prayer is for those of us who are *not* sure, who don't have easy answers; for those of us who no longer have to see things in black or white but are willing to be in areas of gray. (Prayer is also, of course, for those who are "sure," who know their religious tradition is "the way," who do not feel they need to spend time learning the what and the why of other traditions. I used to be in that category. But I'm not sure anymore; I seek teaching wherever I can.)

Prayer is communal. In Jewish circles a minyan, a quorum of ten people, is required for some types of prayer. Christians believe that where two or three are gathered, Christ is present. Temples, shuls, synagogues, churches, chapels, and mosques are all places where believers gather together to pray. Intentional coming together can be intoxicating. Just as the energy that builds when a crowd cheers at a game is exhilarating, so, too, does coming together with the intention of being in the presence of the Holy give our spirits a lift. (A word of caution is in order here. As great as a community gathering for prayer can be, there is sometimes a price that I would call "dogma." If a religious community teaches that to belong we need to believe exclusively in what that tradition holds as true, we are blocked from discovering the secrets of prayer in other traditions.)

Prayer can be communication when there are no words to say. Think about the times you have been with someone experiencing grief. Your words and explanations and carefully worded sympathies were secondary acts to just *being* with the one who was grieving. Your presence was, in fact, your prayer.

Prayer is profoundly about awareness. I have come to recognize that even interruptions can be prayer. I live with my mother, who is in her nineties. It seems that just when I sit down to write, she is at my door, asking me to find her glasses or carry her walker down the stairs or look for her sweater. Sometimes I am absolutely lovely and move at her request. At other times, I express my frustration with not being able to do what I had planned to do. It is then, just when I am my snappiest, my meanest self, that I remember I am writing a book about prayer! About hope! About awareness!

Prayer can be communicating with our whole bodies, our hearts, and our minds. Any serious reflection on prayer needs to consider two terms: *cataphatic* (or *kataphatic*) and *apophatic*. In the ever-present dualism inherent in Greek thought, *cataphatic* refers to our lower nature, which includes our bodily faculties. *Kata* comes from the Greek, signifying something lower, and *phatos* means "spoken" or *phanai*, "to speak" (sometimes meaning "language"). The Greek word *kataphatikos,* meaning "affirmative," comes from *kataphako,* meaning "to make a positive statement."

Cataphatic prayer uses words and images, music and song, actions with hands and feet; it can be very visual, employing symbols and sacraments, rituals and icons. Cynthia Bourgeault in *Centering Prayer and Inner Awakening* tells us that such prayer "engages our reason, memory, imagination, feelings and will."[1] Cataphatic prayers are the most common prayers in many religious traditions, especially in liturgical worship, with its established prayers, ritual gestures, and ritual symbols.

Apophatic prayer, on the other hand, is a prayer beyond words. *Apo*, in the Greek, means "to separate from" or "empty, without content." The Greek word *apophatikos* means "negative" and is derived from *apophemi*, meaning "to say no, to deny."

Rather than being word based, apophatic prayer is an internal process that empties the mind of images and makes intentional space for the presence of God. It is a receptive form of prayer that neither gives something to God (such as praise) nor asks anything of God (such as forgiveness), but rather is a silent opening to whatever God has to offer. Apophatic prayers are an ancient form of meditation used by practitioners from Buddhists to the Desert Fathers and Mothers, from Teresa of Ávila to John of the Cross.

These two contrasting modes of praying represent the wide possibilities on a continuum of prayer styles. In essence, the cataphatic tradition (the "way of affirmation") seeks God by looking at the world; the apophatic tradition (the "way of negation") seeks God by blocking the world out. Both approaches can be helpful, and as you progress through this book, you will discover which one best fits you.

Early on in my journey toward becoming a Sister of St. Joseph, I found out which method *wasn't* for me! Within a month of entering the novitiate, I joined twenty other novices, and we made a thirty-day retreat called Spiritual Exercises of St. Ignatius of Loyola. Ignatius of Loyola (who established the Society of Jesus known as the Jesuits) had realized that there was a pattern in the ways people prayed, and he interviewed everyone he knew to find out what he could about their prayer process. Based on these dialogues, he formalized a prayer methodology that is visually based. Essentially, the pray-er imagines a scene from scripture and puts her- or himself into the picture.

Unfortunately, these cataphatic exercises left me feeling dry; they did not seem to feed me spiritually. However, since this was my first retreat in the convent, I thought that perhaps I just didn't "get it." It was not until six years later, when I learned to meditate in a more formless way, using breath and a mantra, that I experienced a prayer that touched me more deeply.

If you'd like to check out both modes of prayer to see which suits you best, I've included two simple versions you can try. Whichever prayer form is for you, cataphatic or apophatic, it is good to remember Martin Luther's humble request: "Grant that I may not pray alone with the mouth; help me that I may pray from the depths of my heart."

Prayer Exercise

Cataphatic Prayer: Sit in a comfortable position. Open your scripture and choose a story to read. Since most scripture stories do not usually give a great deal of detail, close your eyes and put yourself into the story. Imagine that you are a bystander watching the events. Describe what you see. Notice who is present. What's the weather like? How are people dressed? What do you hear? Can you smell anything? Pay attention to the details. Then watch what the characters do. Are the people aware of you? What is being said? Stay present to the scene for as long as possible. Before you open your eyes, ask yourself whether there is a message there for you. Then open your eyes and take time to reflect on any new insights you have gained.

Apophatic Prayer: Sit (or lie) in a comfortable position. Open your scripture to a favorite passage. Choose a word, a phrase, or a short sentence from this passage. Close your eyes and begin to recite the word (phrase or sentence) out loud. Then speak it softer and softer until it is a whisper. Repeat the word(s) over and over in your mind. Eventually, the meaning of the word(s) may cease to make sense, and you may find yourself wrapped in silence. Stay in the silence as long as possible.

Listening for the Holy

God speaks in the silence of the heart.
Listening is the beginning of prayer.
—*Mother Teresa*

Meditation is the art of listening so that the Divine might speak with us. Its root, *medha*, comes from the Sanskrit word for wisdom.

The concept of meditation was completely foreign to me until I made final vows in my religious order. At that time I met a member of my religious community who had been meditating for years, and a new world opened up to me. As I began to study meditation, I began to understand why this aspect of my training to be a sister had been neglected.

First, meditation is very difficult. It takes commitment. It takes practice. The idea of "going into silence" sounds deceptively simple, but anyone who has tried it will tell you how quickly the wild activity of the mind begins to interfere. And unlike personal prayer that can be done anywhere, anytime, this quieting of the mind and opening of the soul requires an intentional time and space and practice—lots of practice!

Second, meditation can be dangerous. It is, after all, listening to the Holy. It is coming to understand that we are the vehicle through which the Divine communicates. (It can also be dangerous because if we hear something other than what our religious leaders hear, our position becomes tenuous.)

Like prayer, meditation assumes a belief system. Whether practicing Herb Benson's technique taught at the Benson-Henry Institute for Mind Body Medicine in Boston, joining in a communal meditation practice at a Zen center, or chanting with Tibetan monks, practitioners get involved because they believe meditation can affect their lives.

Essentially, meditation is a process of maintaining a relaxed awareness, or more specifically, a brain state of alpha waves. During meditation, our brains shift from beta waves (thirteen or more cycles per second), an awake state with our attention focused on the outer world, to alpha waves (eight to twelve cycles per second), a deep internal state of concentration. Most people can produce, but not maintain, an alpha state by merely shutting their eyes. The point in meditation is to *maintain* the alpha waves.

Our minds are constructed with a marvelous ability to filter out information. For example, let yourself become aware of your breath at this moment. You have been breathing right along as you have been reading, yet you probably were not aware of your breath until you focused on it. Next, become aware of your body. Where are the pressure points where you are touching something? Again, these pressure points have been there all along, but you probably didn't notice them until you shifted your awareness. Go a little further: Think about what has happened to you thus far today. That information is always there, but you are not always aware of it.

This filtering ability provides a protective screen that enables us to maintain our mental health and to function in society. These mental filters hinder an inrush of knowledge that could overwhelm us, and they enable us to focus on the present and the things we need to notice.

Some folks are born with less restrictive filters, and we call them psychics. One of my religious sisters, Eusebius, was born with what the Irish call a veil. The veil (or caul) is a membrane that covers the entire head of a newborn child. Irish midwives knew to pinch the tip of the membrane and remove it in one piece. When the membrane was removed this way, it was thought the infant would have "the sight." Eusebius (who used to play on her name and say "you see by us") was born with a double veil. The first time I met her, she looked at me and said, "The nineteenth of December!" I nodded and confirmed that this was indeed the date of my birth. That information was just present for her.

Others born with less restricted filters are not so fortunate, and many are diagnosed with some sort of mental illness. Some try to remove their filters with drugs, but drugs cause the barriers to come down quickly and trigger a rapid influx of information that can cause problems. And, needless to say, the physical state related to being high cannot be maintained.

The discipline of meditation allows the barriers to come down gradually. The slowing down of our minds and bodies gives us time to become used to the influx of more information, and our consciousness can expand in an unhurried process to the alpha state—or even to what some refer to as enlightenment or a mystical experience.

What meditation does is clear our lens. By expanding our awareness, we can look at our world—and what we perceive to be reality—through new eyes. Deepak Chopra speaks about "preconceived cognitive commitments," that is, early decisions we make as we generalize from our particular situation. Experiments have indicated self-restrictive behavior exists in the natural world. Newborn fish, for example, were put into tanks divided by a clear plastic wall. When the divider was later removed, the fish continued to swim in only their half, as if the divider were still present. When fruit flies were raised in a closed jar and the cover later removed, the flies remained in the jar, unaware that they could leave.

It is no different with humans. Take the story of Columbus. When he visited the Caribbean Islands for the first time, the native people didn't see a large ship. There was nothing in their world that would have made it possible for them to believe such a large craft could exist. Instead, they saw a floating island with tall, defoliated trees and hairy creatures. We've all had our own experiences of "preconceived cognitive commitments." I think of my childhood perception about my world. Because my family and friends were all Catholic, I applied that knowledge to everyone. I thought the world was Catholic, even though I was raised in a town that was 80 percent Jewish!

When we apply our preconceived notions to the sacred, we end up blocking our full experience. The relaxed awareness of meditation allows us to become conscious of these preconceptions, which in turn opens us to a greater sense of both reality and freedom.

Some associate meditation with mystics, as if meditation were only for those who are "spiritually enlightened." In truth, mystics are essentially women and men who take listening seriously. The term *mystic* comes from the Greek word *muo*, which means "hidden or concealed." And that touches on the core of the mystical experience: It is "hidden" from logical, verbal explanations. When a mystic attempts to explain to someone who has not had the experience of the ineffable, words fail, and it may appear that the mystic is "hiding" something. In reality, the mystic is attempting to explain that which cannot be described, only experienced. A Hindu story captures this dilemma:

There was once a pond with lots of tadpoles. One of the tadpoles developed into a frog and went off to discover life outside the pond. She missed her friends and returned to visit the tadpoles. The little tadpoles were eager to hear of her adventures outside the pond.

"What is it like out there?"

"Well," she said, "out there I breathe air, not water."

"Air? What is air?" asked the tadpoles.

"Air is like water; it surrounds everything but it is not wet," she replied.

"Not wet? How can you breathe what is not wet? What else is it like?"

"Well, the land is hard, not soft like the bottom of the pond," she said.

"Hard, how can land be hard? Land is always soft. You must be crazy!"

The tadpoles could not understand. The young frog eventually stopped trying to speak of the outside world and simply said to the tadpoles, "You'll just have to see for yourselves!"

If meditation is something you have shied away from—either because it is outside the boundaries of your religious tradition, or because you haven't known quite where to begin—I offer a simple meditation exercise that you might want to try.

Meditation Exercise

If you are new to meditation, I recommend beginning with a five-minute time period. Setting a timer helps (as long as you can't hear it ticking). Eventually, work your way up to thirty minutes. Always allow enough time to come back to yourself gently at the end of your meditation. You can try either a cataphatic or an apophatic form, or both.

Cataphatic Meditation: Choose an object that has religious significance for you (such as a Jewish *chai* symbol signifying life, a Christian cross, or a Muslim crescent moon). Simply stare at it, thinking about what the symbol means to you, how it entered your life, what it reminds you of. Then let go of your thoughts and focus your eyes on your symbol. Relax into the symbol and let everything fade away.

Apophatic Meditation: Get in a comfortable position, preferably with your spine straight, and begin to breathe slowly. Concentrate on your breathing. Be aware of the air flowing into your nostrils and then out. Keep your attention on your breath: in and out, in and out. When your mind wanders—and it will—bring it gently back to focusing on your breath.

Being with the Holy

There come times when I have nothing more to tell God. If I were
to continue to pray in words, I would have to repeat what I have
already said. At such times it is wonderful to say to God, "May I
be in Thy presence, Lord? I have nothing more to say to Thee, but
I do love to be in Thy presence."

—O. Hallesby

I like to think of contemplation as the "ah" of an "ah-hah!" moment,
the moment when we "get it." Contemplation is the discipline of going
past thought, past concepts, past images into a deep silence where the
functions of the body slow down while the mind expands. Breathing,
blood pressure, heart rate, and general metabolism decrease as conscious awareness increases. Contemplation is called a variety of names:
samadhi for Hindus, ayin for Jews, san'mai or one-pointedness for
Buddhists, prayer of quiet for Christians, and fana for Muslims.

In essence, the goal of every form of contemplation is to be able
to concentrate your mind on a single thing and keep it there, so your
whole body and mind can be at peace from distractions and be at rest.
Contemplation is another of those "almost impossible to describe" experiences, and the closest I can come is to compare it to another experience. Think of the feeling you get when you are holding an infant,
and she lets go and falls asleep in your arms. You just stay there. You
do not want to move and break the spell. You do not want the feeling
to end. That is something of the state of contemplation.

The qualities of the altered state of contemplation are four: ineffable, noetic, transient, and joyful. Ineffable means that the experience
is incapable of being expressed; it can only be experienced. Noetic suggests that the experience has a definitive cognitive or intellectual con-

tent accompanied by a sense of authority, a realization of true knowledge. *Transient* suggests that this peak experience is not permanent, but passes with time. *Joyful* suggests that we understand that we are being moved by a power deeper than ourselves and that, in the words of Julian of Norwich, "All will be well."

One of the classic texts for Christians on contemplation, *The Cloud of Unknowing*, was written in the fourteenth century. The text is written in Middle English, which suggests that it was intended for laypeople, since the clergy read texts in Latin. The author's anonymity suggests that the text may have been written by a woman. In 1974, William Meninger, a Trappist monk, found a copy of the text in the library of the monastery in Spencer, Massachusetts. He devoured the book and began to teach the experience of contemplation from the Christian tradition through the practice of centering prayer. A year later, Thomas Keating, who was Meninger's abbot, and fellow monk M. Basil Pennington joined him. Thanks to their books and teachings, centering prayer is now one of the most popular forms of prayer for Christians. In essence, centering prayer is an intentional opening to God's presence that gives us the opportunity to move into the rich experience of contemplation.

Other intense life experiences, such as art, can bring us to the altered state of consciousness of contemplation. A symphony, a painting, or a dance can move us in ways that the ordinariness of our days seldom does. Being in nature can also bring us to such a place. So can physical intimacy. (More on that later!)

However, it is important to recognize that a state of contemplation is not intended to be a permanent escape to a better place. Contemplation is the *before* part that leads to an expanded sense of the sacred, but there needs to be an after, a return to a full life. There is a Buddhist expression, "after Nirvana … the laundry." In other words, the true contemplative experiences the ecstasy and yet still does the mundane activities of physical life—just with a new perspective.

Contemplation Exercise

Contemplation is a paradox. It is an action and a gift. It is the result of a spiritual practice or it just is. It can happen to anyone at any time and any place, but it cannot be programmed. It is a gift given to us. We can put ourselves in a stance, we can meditate, we can pray—and contemplation may be our experience or it may not.

The simplest practice I know to allow an experience in contemplation is to gaze into the face of a beloved. Just be there. Wallow in the love. And remember, nothing lasts forever. Just as water evaporates and snow melts, so too will contemplation come to a natural end.

If you are interested in exploring contemplation further, you might want to try this simple centering prayer exercise. Start with a five-minute period and increase your time as you are able:

1. Find a quiet place where you can sit comfortably.
2. Choose a word that will help you focus, something that will help you be mindful of love or grace or spirit.
3. Take slow, deep breaths as you relax.
4. Ask that you be open, and then begin speaking your word.
5. Gradually, let the word fall away and be with the holy presence.

6. When you find your mind wandering, repeat your prayer word again until you are recentered.
7. Continue until you are ready to move gently back into the realities of your day.

Prayer, meditation, and contemplation are foundations in every religious tradition. The paradox is that even within widely different practices there is a similarity. Like other human experiences, we all eat, yet we eat different foods. For some taro root is a staple; for others, it's wheat or rice, cassava or potato. We all drink, yet our chosen drinks are varied. We may prefer yak butter tea or coffee, water, or milk.

In the same way, there are multiple ways of experiencing the Holy. As you explore the vehicles of prayer, meditation, and contemplation, as you find your own way of seeking the Divine, know that you are a part of a long tradition of spiritual seekers. As Ralph H. Blum teaches in *The Book of Runes,* on the spiritual journey one is always on the first step.

Secret 2

Your Body Is a Source of Energy for Prayer

The wonderful beauty of prayer is that the opening of our heart is as natural as the opening of a flower. To let a flower open and bloom, it is only necessary to let it BE; so if we simply ARE, if we become and remain still and silent, our heart cannot but be open, the Spirit cannot but pour through into the whole of our being. It is for this we have been created.

—*Dom John Main*

I know folks who are confident that they have a right to address the Holy One—the force, or love, from which we all come. And I know others for whom the idea of having a personal conversation with God is a foreign concept. For many, the core question about prayer may well boil down to this: "Can I really be intimate with the Divine?"

There are two primary ways we approach the Divine: *transcendent* and *immanent*. *Transcendent* refers to the idea of the Holy as other, independent from all of creation, a force or energy beyond the cosmos, not limited to it or by it. *Immanent*, on the other hand, refers to the Holy that is in and with all of creation. A transcendent experience will bring us out of ourselves, and an immanent experience will bring us into ourselves.

The way I like to differentiate between the two is this: If you believe that the Divine is transcendent, then you are always within God. If you believe God is immanent, then, like the Kabbalists, you believe everyone has a spark of the Divine within.

Perhaps you have heard the story about God wanting to be in the world after having created humankind. But God needed to be in a place somewhat hidden so that humans would learn in the very seeking of the Divine. It is said that God decided to become imbedded within the human heart.

This immanence is what Ursuline Sister Nancy Malone is describing when she writes about "intimacy with myself and with God."[1] I believe that when we are intimate with ourselves—when we truly know ourselves, when we connect with the yearnings of our hearts—we connect with the sacred; that knowing ourselves is the beginning of prayer.

If we start with the premise that praying is the process of creating a relationship with that which we cannot see, then how we are in relationship with what is *visible*—ourselves—intimately affects how we are in relationship with the *invisible*. In other words, if we wish to be in touch with the Holy that is immanent, we need to be in touch with ourselves. Knowing ourselves is the first step to being in communication with the Creator. Interiority is the beginning of prayer.

To truly grasp this concept, we need to understand a little more about how we are linked to the larger universe. Stick with me for a moment—I promise not to lead you into a quagmire of quantum physics, but rather to a closer look at the secrets the universe holds for our prayer life.

The Principle of Interiority

You are absolutely unique, just like everyone else.

—Margaret Mead

The Magen (or shield) of David is one of the most recognized symbols of Judaism. It is composed of two overlapping, equilateral triangles, the tip of one pointing upward and the tip of the other pointing downward. The spiritual significance of this is summed up in the phrase, "As above, so below." Basically, this means that the laws of the physical world apply both to the cosmos (above) and the atoms (below). It is also interpreted to mean that the laws of the invisible spiritual world that we cannot see reflect the visible world we can see. Parents have long understood this idea when it comes to raising children: Children imitate what they see their parents doing—as above, so below.

In a fascinating turnaround of this phrase, cultural historian Thomas Berry proposes, "As below, so above." In essence, this means that the way things function below is the same way things function above, that by studying the below we can see the above. Taking this one step further, Berry describes three inherent principles of the universe that apply equally to both the visible reality of our lives and the invisible nature of the cosmos. And therein lies the link to prayer: Each principle suggests how we relate to the universe, and how the universe relates to us. Each principle suggests an entryway into the direct experience of cosmic presence.

Briefly, the three principles are: *interiority*, *differentiation*, and *communion*. *Interiority* refers to maintaining our integrity. Every living thing—plant, animal, or human—needs to be itself. *Differentiation* refers to the extraordinary variety, distinctiveness, and uniqueness of everything in universe. No two things are completely alike. *Communion* refers to our ability to relate to other people and things *because* of our integrity and our difference.

Together these principles create the grounds for the inner attraction of things for one another—even our "attraction" to God. In subsequent chapters, we'll look at the principles of differentiation and communion, but I want to start with the principle of interiority because it links so directly to the beginning of prayer.

Think of an oak tree, standing tall and majestic, with its strong branches and shapely leaves. It would be silly to expect this natural architectural wonder to suddenly bear fruit, or lay eggs, or migrate with the seasons. It is an oak tree, and it needs to be itself, in all its "tree-ness," and to honor its particular place in creation. In the same way, water needs to be itself; birds, bears, and beetles need to be themselves; we need to be ourselves. When we are being the best self that we can be, not trying to be anything else, then we contribute to the whole.

This is the essence of interiority: knowing who we are and maintaining our integrity. There is a story I love that humorously expresses the value of being ourselves:

> A hard-working young chief executive officer of a corporation took his family to a Caribbean island. One day he rented a fishing boat that was owned and captained by a delightful man. The CEO was impressed with the cleanliness of the boat, the care the captain took of his clients, and the knowledge he demonstrated of areas where fish would be plentiful. The CEO's family had a wonderful day.

Impressed with the industry that the young captain displayed, the CEO inquired whether the captain had thought of buying another boat.

"No, I have not," he replied. "I really love my life. I have three children and a beautiful wife. I sing in a band for the tourists at night. They tip very well. What would be the point of getting another boat?"

"Well," the CEO responded, "you could catch more fish to sell and take more tourists out on a bigger boat. You would make lots of money, which you could give to your children. And you could retire in comfort."

The captain wondered what he would do when he retired.

The CEO quickly replied, "You could spend the rest of your time doing things you enjoy, like fishing, boating, playing with your grandchildren, singing at the clubs."

"Oh," remarked the captain, "you mean I could live as I do now."

As anthropologist Margaret Mead so eloquently stated, each of us is "absolutely unique, just like everyone else." By understanding our values, traditions, culture, aspirations, and competencies, by being more conscious of who we are and what our choices and actions create for us, we strengthen our interiority.

Interiority also means acknowledging and honoring the sacred within us. Every entity in the universe, whether an atom, a mountain, a flower, or a person, contains within its being the entire depth of the universe, as William Blake's poem "Auguries of Innocence" articulates so eloquently:

To see a World in a Grain of Sand
And Heaven in a Wild Flower
Hold Infinity in the palm of your hand
And Eternity in an hour

The bottom line is that we need to know the full range of ourselves—our physical bodies and our sacred essence—for our prayers to have integrity. There are multiple ways of learning about ourselves. We might take personality tests, such as the Myers-Briggs or the Enneagram, or we might consult a career counselor, or take an aptitude test, and so forth. We might seek advice from our friends to help us to recognize our strengths and weaknesses. Have you heard about a process called the "I god you" way? Basically, this is when someone who loves you—a friend, a confessor, a spiritual director, an *anam cara* ("soul friend" in Irish), someone who can see you with the eye of the Divine— helps to reveal your self to you. Even our enemies can be important in helping us know ourselves: They can tell us things about ourselves that others may not wish to expose for fear of hurting us.

Another way we understand ourselves is by becoming aware of what brings us joy, of what gives us bliss. We live in a culture that tells us we will have bliss if we use a certain product, travel to a certain place, or earn a lot of money. Women are often programmed to believe that bliss comes by creating bliss for others. I think of my friend Barbara: When her husband died, she realized that she had been so concerned with pleasing him that she did not even know what music she liked! True bliss comes from identifying what it is we really want to do with this rare and precious life we are living.

In whatever ways we seek to know ourselves, interiority is the beginning of prayer.

> **An Interiority Prayer Exercise**
> Go to a comfortable, quiet place and recall the times in your life when you truly felt bliss. Retrieve every part of the memory in as much detail as possible. Stay with that memory. Then reflect on how you can reconnect with some of that experience in the circumstances you now find yourself. Trust your feelings and let your reflection become a prayer of gratitude for your true self.

Your Body Matters

Prayer requires more of the heart than of the tongue.

—Adam Clarke

To know ourselves, we start, of course, with the body. As long as we exist on this plane, the only way we can go to God, the only way we experience the Holy, is through our body. When it comes to things of the spirit, our bodies do indeed matter.

Yet for many of us—especially women—our bodies have been censored. I was raised in a third-generation Irish Catholic family where bodily functions were never discussed and certainly the word *sex* was never spoken. Once when my grandfather came up behind my grandmother as she was washing dishes and gave her a hug, she exclaimed in a loud voice, "James! The children!"

In the time and place I grew up, shame and ignorance were the two primary means of dealing with the taboo topic of the body. Once as a youngster of about eight years, I scratched my "private area" in front of my aunt Catherine. In a severe voice she scolded me and told me never to touch "there" because it was vulgar. I had no idea what vulgar was, but I knew it was bad. The facts of life were passed on with a single talk by my mother. My sister and I were so embarrassed that we assured her that we knew all about "it," when in fact we knew nothing. I was about sixteen before I understood how babies were conceived.

Incidents like this enforced a numbness in me about my body and my sexuality. As I grew older, I encountered different kinds of oppression of my body. When I wanted to earn a master's degree at a Catholic theology school, the shape of my body got in the way. If my body had had the shape of Jesus, in other words, a male body, I could have hoped for ordination. But since my body had the shape of Mary, I could not.

As a young novice, I had heard about locked bookcases within a convent that contained forbidden books that were viewed as potentially dangerous. Among them were the writings of mystics and texts that spoke about knowing God experientially, not merely believing in God. These Gnostics, as they were called, believed that it was more important to *know* God than to know *about* God.

When I finally began to read these texts, I realized that these mystics seemed to tap into an internal energy in the body to fuel their prayer practices. A body not separate from mind, soul, and spirit, but rather infused in some mysterious way with life energy. A body sacred in itself. Although in my tradition I had been taught that we are created in the image and likeness of the Divine, I had been blocked from knowing my body, and I had never been conscious of the life force within me. I was in my late twenties before I even heard the word *chakras*.

In the Hindu tradition, there are seven energy centers throughout the body that are responsible for the condition of the mind, body, and spirit. These energy points are called chakras, and they ascend from the base of the spine in this sequence:

root chakra (sacrum plexus)

sacral chakra (hypogastric plexus)

solar plexus chakra (celiac plexus)

heart chakra (cardiac plexus)

throat chakra (throat or pharyngeal plexus)

brow chakra (pituitary and Third Eye at the center of the
forehead)

crown chakra (pineal and top of head)

When we are ignorant of the existence of chakras, we can experience an energy crisis. It's rather like being in a house in Boston (or any place that experiences severe drops in temperature during the winter season) and having no idea where the thermostat is located. The oil burner is in the cellar, but you don't know how to turn the heater on. There you sit with lots of reserve energy, but it is not available to you. It is the same way with our ignorance of our energy within. If we are unaware that such an energy supply exists, we are at a severe disadvantage.

When we begin to understand that this very energy is our connection to God, we can tap into a new resource to fuel our prayer practice. To put it another way, the *immanent* energy in our bodies is identical to the *transcendent* energy of creation. When we are conscious of this shared life force, we begin to understand that the very energy of our bodies is a connection to God. This energy is available to everyone. To consciously use this energy enriches our lives and deepens our prayer.

When I became aware of the energy released by the chakras, my prayer life changed. When I aligned my energy with that of the Holy One, my prayer gained in integrity because my thoughts and words became one. I finally began to know the difference between believing in God and *knowing* God.

Though I do not have a head for physics, I am intrigued by Einstein's formula $E = mc^2$. Here is my translation of this formula: energy = mass (*physical body*) x consciousness doubled (*awareness*).

Or, to put it another way, when we put our bodies and our developing consciousnesses together, we can accomplish much. We can literally make something out of nothing. And that is one of the secrets of prayer: The energy in our bodies is a source of energy for our prayers.

If you've read about or studied the chakras, you already know a bit of what I am talking about. If the idea of chakras is new to you—maybe even a bit suspect or too "New Agey"—don't take my word for it: Try it. I believe your prayer life, too, will change.

A Chakra Prayer Exercise

One of the easiest ways to experience the energy of the lower chakra is through a simple visualization exercise.

1. Choose a quiet place and sit in a comfortable position, either on the floor or in a chair. (It is important to keep your back straight. This posture prevents your body from becoming sluggish or sleepy and facilitates the energy rising up your spine.)
2. Set a timer for five minutes so you won't be distracted by wondering how much time has passed while you focus on this exercise.
3. Close your eyes and place your hands, open and facing up, on your thighs. Breathe naturally.

4. Picture white light coiled into a ball at the base of your spine. See this light unravel and move up your spinal column and neck, until it reaches the crown of your head. Hold this image in your mind's eye for as long as you can or until the timer shuts off.

The Flow of Energy

> Only in prayer do we achieve that complete and harmonious assembly of body, mind and spirit which gives the frail human reed its unshakable strengths.
>
> —*Dr. Alexis Carrel*

One way to understand chakras is to think of your body energy as flowing up and down your spinal column. When the energy flows freely, you are in balance and can experience a sense of calm and well-being. When the energy is blocked, when it does not flow freely, you are out of balance. You might feel anxious, distracted, disconnected. If the energy is blocked at the base of your spine, you may be frightened and overly concerned with physical survival; your concentration will be on your safety. A blockage a bit higher up might signify a fear of healthy intimacy or a preoccupation with gaining genital gratification. If energy is blocked further up the spine, you may be consumed with a desire to control others, to dominate situations.

Any of these blockages can sabotage your spiritual journey. It is only as your energy flows up your spine to the higher chakras that you will be able to have the energy available to look beyond your own needs to the concerns of others. As the energy continues to flow, you will be more able to access love, compassion, insight, and communion with the Divine.

First Chakra: The Root Chakra

The lower chakras are energy points all about your individual self, starting with the basic issue of security. The root chakra or security center (*muladhara*) is associated with the perineum, the point between the anus and the sex organs at the base of the spine. It is the seat of what is called *kundalini*, from the Sanskrit word meaning "snake" or "serpent power." Imagine that this energy is like a snake coiled at the bottom of the trunk of your body. When it is stirred, think of it rising through the chakras above it, moving like a snake up the line of the spine.

Gratitude is the key to prayer and the key that unlocks the energy we hold within our body. Thus a prayer at the first chakra would be one of gratitude for the safety and security we experience in our lives *even if we are feeling unsafe and insecure*! This may sound inconsistent, but bear with me. The energy will rise *only* when we believe that we are safe and secure. As we believe, so shall it be. Or in the words of the Master Jesus in Matthew 8:13, "Be it done for you as you have believed." Think of this as a way of praying your way into a new way of being. Pray the words of gratitude daily: *Today I give thanks for the security and safety that is in my life.*

Second Chakra: The Sacral Chakra

Next in importance to our drive for self-preservation is our sexual drive, and this is the energy of the second chakra. It is totally related to pleasure, especially in the areas of food and sex. The sacral chakra (*svadhisthana*) is associated with our genitalia and governs our sexuality and reproduction (and, many would add, our creativity).

The energy in this chakra is extremely seductive. There are some who never move their energy any further than this; their whole lives revolve around satisfying themselves, and pleasure becomes the aim of their existence. The sacral chakra can also frighten us. This energy in the female body appears to be of particular concern in patriarchal cultures where there is a concerted effort to use sexuality as a means of control. The Reverend Dr. Carter Heyward of the Episcopal Divinity School in Cambridge, Massachusetts, once remarked that if the energy spent on trying to hide our sexuality was loosed on the world, a revolution for justice would be minutes away.

This second chakra presents a paradox. We live in a culture that presents sex as the only means of intimacy. There are, however, a number of ways of intimately relating to others without becoming genitally active. Celibate or not, we cannot ignore the power of the second chakra. *Not* to experience this chakra's energy would restrict our emotional development. The second chakra is our energy source for *any* processes of generativity and creativity. We can move this energy by sharing it with another (as in intercourse), or we can move this energy ourselves. It is a delicate balance to learn how to walk this razor's edge, to tame the seductive energy of the second chakra.

A prayer at the second chakra would be another prayer of gratitude, this time for the energy we have for relationships, first with ourselves and then with others: *Today I give thanks for the energy I have for relationships. May I continue to be blessed with loved ones in my life.*

Third Chakra: The Solar Plexus Chakra

The third chakra (*manipura*) is associated with our solar plexus and is connected with our personal power. I called it our "power point," not in the sense of computers, but rather as the energy we tap into when we exert control over our lives. Energy on this level is proactive, not passive. It is energy for decisions. The solar plexus is associated with our perceptions of freedom, control, and the power to be ourselves.

When we feel powerless, critical of ourselves, or insecure, we become jealous. We feel isolated and take a defensive stance, and a need to oppress those who are different from us emerges. The energy from this center can encourage us to put ourselves in positions that dominate others.

However, when we are in touch with and comfortable with our personal power, we remove the possibility of jealousy. When we feel at ease with ourselves, we do not need to be in competition with others. It is only then that we can gaze at others with awe, with the understanding that they are truly our sisters and brothers.

Humility is the key to understanding the energy of the third chakra. True humility is the ability to acknowledge our gifts and likewise the gifts of others; to acknowledge our reliance on other members of earth's community. It's when we think we are "in charge" that problems arise. Any time we place ourselves over and above another on the basis of intelligence, wealth, position, or the like is an obstacle on our path. Humble people are those who understand the human condition, especially their own. Humility is an approach to life that says, "I don't have all the answers, and I need your contribution."

A prayer at the third chakra would be one of humility for the gift we ourselves are, and gratitude for the gift others are to us: *Today I give thanks for my gifts and for the giftedness I see in others.*

The energy of the next four chakras, the upper chakras, is open to us only after we have experienced the energy of these three lower chakras. When our survival and safety needs are met, when our sexual energies are directed in a satisfying way, and when we are secure in our own personal power, then we are ready to reach out to others in a healing way. We are able to be compassionate, open to wisdom, and responsive to the embrace of the Divine. Our prayer is no longer primarily concerned with ourselves; our communication with the Divine begins to take over, and our journey becomes a bit clearer.

Fourth Chakra: The Heart Chakra

The fourth chakra (*anahata*), located in the center of the chest, is called the heart chakra. When I first read about the heart chakra, I could not find anything in my own tradition that seemed to relate to this energy. Then I started to see, as if for the first time, pictures and statues of Jesus and of his mother, Mary, with hearts exposed. The images showed flames leaping upward and light streaming outward from the centers of their chests. Catholics refer to these figures as portraits of the Sacred Heart of Jesus and the Sacred Heart of Mary. These images, going as far back as the early Middle Ages, had been there all along for me.

Unlike the first three chakras, which are focused within, the energy from the fourth chakra moves outward. The commandment to love our neighbors as ourselves typifies the movement of heart chakra energy. A prayer at the fourth chakra would be one of gratitude for the love of others and a prayer that we will love others as we love ourselves: *Today I give thanks for the love I have for myself and pray that it might increase the love I have for others.*

Fifth Chakra: The Throat Chakra

The fifth chakra (*visuddha*) is located in the throat area and is considered the chakra of compassion. The throat chakra is linked with the concept of abundance, as experienced in "Ask and you shall receive."

A prayer at the fifth chakra would be one of gratitude for the compassion that has been shown to us and the compassion we are able to exhibit to others: *Today I give thanks for the compassion I receive and share with others.*

Sixth Chakra: The Brow Chakra

The sixth chakra (*ajna*) is located in the middle of the forehead between the eyes. It is referred to as the Third Eye or brow chakra, and its focus is on wisdom or insight. If you close your eyes and picture someone you love, and then place your finger on the part of your forehead where you "see" that person, that is your Third Eye. For Christians, this is reaffirmed in the scripture, "The eye is the lamp of your body" (Luke 11:34).

In the brow chakra our unconscious motivations become clear. Awareness of the "big picture"—including spiritual enlightenment and psychic phenomenon—is associated with this chakra. A prayer at the sixth chakra would be one of gratitude for the knowledge and understandings we have internalized: *Today I give thanks for the insights I have been given; may I use them for the healing of the world.*

Seventh Chakra: The Crown Chakra

The seventh chakra is called the crown chakra (*sahasrara*). This energy field is a place of knowing and is located on the top of the head, the place on the skull that is soft in infancy. Many people also believe that at death the soul leaves the body from this location.

Several faith traditions recognize the importance of the crown through ritual head coverings: Jewish men (and now some women) often wear a small skullcap (called a yarmulke or *kippah*) on the top of the head, covering the crown. The pope wears a white skullcap called a *pileolus*; cardinals have red caps, bishops, violet, and prelates, black. Monks from the Middle Ages onward, rather than covering this area, often shaved the top of the head to remind them to be conscious of where to focus their energies. Both Hinduism and Christianity have a tradition of tonsure (from the Latin word *tonsus*, meaning "to shear").

Being conscious of the crown chakra keeps us aware of the energy that reaches toward the Divine; some even refer to this flow of energy as "intercourse with the Divine," knowing that we are one with the Holy. A prayer at the seventh chakra would be one of gratitude for the consciousness we have of the Divine in our lives: *Today I give thanks for the awareness I have of how the Holy is present in my life.*

As you become alert to your energy centers, you will not only know where your energy gets stuck, but also how your energy flows. When you access the energy that is available in your body, your prayer life, your communication with God, will gain integrity. And you will have a new appreciation for the gift of your body as a tool for communicating with the Divine.

Prayer in Motion

Accustom yourself gradually to carry Prayer into all your daily occupation—speak, act, work in peace, as if you were in prayer.

—*François Fénelon*

We humans seem to have a hard time staying still. The next time you observe two people in conversation, observe their hands. Their gestures will probably be as expressive as their words! In 1959, anthropologist Edward T. Hall wrote a book titled *The Silent Language* about each culture's unique patterns that are passed on without words. Hand gestures in particular communicate immediately, as this traditional story humorously reveals:

> About a century ago, the Pope decided that all the Jews had to leave Rome. Naturally, there was a big uproar from the Jewish community, so the Pope made a deal. He would have a religious debate with a member of the Jewish community. If the Jews won, the Jews could stay. If the Pope won, they would have to leave.
>
> The Jews realized that they had no choice, so they selected an old man named Moishe to represent them. Moishe asked for one addition to the debate: to make it more interesting, neither side would be allowed to talk. The Pope agreed.
>
> The day of the great debate came. They sat opposite one another for a full minute before the Pope raised his hand over his head and showed three fingers. Moishe looked back at him and raised one finger. The Pope waved his fingers in a circle around his head. Moishe pointed to the ground where he sat. The Pope pulled out bread and a glass of wine. Moishe pulled out an apple.
>
> The Pope stood up and said, "I give up; this man is too good. The Jews can stay."
>
> An hour later, the cardinals surrounded the Pope and asked him what happened. The Pope said, "First, I held up three fingers to represent the Trinity. He responded by holding up one finger to remind me that there was still one God common to both of our religions. Then I waved my finger around to show that God was all around us. He responded by pointing to the ground and showing that God was right here with us. I

pulled out the bread and wine to show him how God absolves us from our sins. He pulled out an apple to remind me of the original sin. He had an answer for everything. What could I do?"

Meanwhile, the Jewish community had gathered around Moishe, "Well," said Moishe, "first he said to me that the Jews had three days to get out of the city. I told him that not one of us was leaving. Then he told me that the whole city would be cleared of Jews. I told him no; that we were staying right here."

"And then?" asked a woman.

"I don't know," said Moishe, "he took out his lunch, so I took out mine."

While this story is certainly poking fun at misinterpretation, it is a reality that we rely on gestures for multiple levels of communication. Hand gestures are also found in every religious tradition and are especially articulated and taught consciously in the Hindu and Buddhist faiths. The teaching is that by curling, stretching, and touching fingers and hands, energy flow is guided throughout the body, particularly to the brain. The brain then responds to certain parts of the body/mind.

In Hinduism, a mudra, which means "seal" in Sanskrit, is a symbolic gesture or position of the hands that identifies a deeper meaning. For example, this is a mudra to encourage serenity: Sit with a straight spine; rest your left palm on your left thigh; raise your right hand to shoulder level, elbow at your side and palm facing outward.

Whenever you see a holy picture or sculpture from the Hindu or Buddhist tradition, notice the hands. A mudra gives significance to a sculptural image, a dance movement, or a meditative pose, intensifying its effectiveness. It is a healing art of symbolical gestures through which invisible forces may operate on the earthly sphere. Mudras attune the body to a greater consciousness of the Divine both within and without.

After learning about these "prayers in motion," I began to be more aware of the hand gestures in my own tradition. The *fiat* or *ad sum* position is often seen in statues of Mary at the Annunciation, when she was told that she was to bear a child of God. Mary kneels with both of her palms turned upward. Statues and pictures of Jesus always demonstrate hand gestures or sign language of the soul, as it is often called. Whenever Catholics enter their church, they dip their hands into a basin of holy water and make a sign of a cross over themselves.

In his autobiography, *I Am Spock*, Leonard Nimoy of *Star Trek* fame said that he based his Vulcan salute (the right hand up, palm facing outward, holding the thumb separately, the index and forefinger together, and the ring and little finger together) on a blessing performed by the Jewish rabbis representing the Hebrew letter Shin: ש. The letter Shin here stands for *Shaddai*, meaning "Almighty God," and has mystical significance in Judaism.

Muslims also use a variety of hand gestures along with the kneeling and bowing posture as they prostrate themselves during prayer, and it is believed that ritual hand postures may have eventually contributed to the development of the mudras of Indian classical dance.

When I attended the Black Catholic Institute at Xavier University in New Orleans, I had the joy of studying with Glenn Parker, a Catholic priest now stationed in Georgia. Glenn's mother was a minister in the Holiness Christian Church, where church services include dancing. When Glenn celebrated liturgy, his movements flowed, and he would often dance at meaningful parts of the service.

Knowing that I had never before seen a priest dance in church, the other students explained to me that dance often occurs in African

American Catholic churches when either the priest or the people "get happy," that is, when they experience the spirit of the Divine and the joy flows from their bodies as dance. I would suggest that this is yet another example of a mudra, or prayer in motion.

And then there is prayer in motion in the form of walking—a pilgrimage. Many religious traditions embrace the concept of pilgrimage. Muslims make a pilgrimage, or haj, to Mecca, Saudi Arabia, considered to be the holiest city on earth, for it houses the Kaaba, a small cubic building believed to have been built by Abraham. For Armenian Christians, haj means a pilgrimage to Jerusalem, the city where Jesus died. For Jewish people, it means an aliyah to Jerusalem, a return to the land of their ancestors. For Tibetan Buddhists, it means a pilgrimage to Lhasa, the ancient home of the Dalai Lama. For Carmelite nuns, it means a trip to Ávila, Spain, where Teresa was born. For many Christians, it is walking along El Camino de Santiago de Compostela (the Way of St. James of Compostela in Spain). For many Catholics, it could be a visit to Rome and Vatican City, the home of the pope. For astronauts, it might be a voyage to view earth from outer space. For environmentalists, it might mean a trip to a place of natural beauty, such as a national park. A friend of mine, Cookie, considers her trip to her ancestral home in Poland to visit the Nazi concentration camp of Auschwitz-Birkenau a pilgrimage.

A pilgrimage can be a community experience taken with others, or it can be taken alone. But it is always a commitment to a belief in something and a journey to be more in touch with the sacred in our lives.

Some pilgrimages are long—to distant cities or countries. Others are symbolic, such as the labyrinth. A labyrinth is similar in structure and use to the medicine wheel of Native Americans and the never-ending circles of my Irish (Celtic) ancestors. It is not a maze; it has no dead ends and is not meant to be a puzzle, but a process. The labyrinth is meant to be walked as a pilgrimage or quest, a journey taken with the hope of becoming closer to the Divine. Walking through a labyrinth becomes a metaphor for change, movement, direction, transformation, and patience.

No matter where we take our pilgrimage, we are on a path. In reality, we are on a haj every day of our lives. If we are aware, our movement, our life itself, is a prayer. Prayer in motion—whether it be going on a pilgrimage, walking a labyrinth, choosing a mudra posture or gesture, or dancing in church—makes us aware of the Holy in the human body. Body movements and hand gestures communicate immediately our intent, making the invisible visible, pouring prayer out of our hearts into our bodies, and flowing toward God.

A "Prayer in Motion" Exercise

Consider the mudras in your religious tradition. Perhaps it is the way people raise their hands or grasp each others' hands before they pray. Perhaps it is something more formalized or ritualized. As you pray today, think of a hand gesture or body movement that would reflect what is on your mind and in your heart. Let your silent movement be your prayer as you let it flow out of your body toward God.

A Sacred Feast

> Prayer opens the heart to God, and it is the means
> by which the soul, though empty, is filled by God.
> —*John Bunyan*

Another way our bodies can aid us in prayer is through fasting. By fasting, I don't mean dieting. I'm talking about limiting our intake so we can be more sensitive to our bodies, more conscious of our choices. Fasting from food, or abstaining from certain types of food, is a discipline that can make us more aware of our bodies, our cravings, and our compulsions. It can clear our minds for prayer and meditation and open our hearts in compassion—especially for those who are without the basic necessities for life. And it can bring us into a more intimate relationship with the very source for whom we hunger.

Fasting appears in every spiritual tradition. In Islam, fasting during Ramadan is one of the five pillars that are the foundations of Muslim life. Muslims fast during the holy month of Ramadan from sunrise to sunset, abstaining from food, water, tobacco, and sexual intimacy. (This is relatively simple during the winter season, when the sun appears for only a few hours during the day. But since Muslims follow a lunar calendar, Ramadan occurs ten days earlier each year. When Ramadan occurs during the summer months, with sunrise at 4 a.m. and sunset at 10 p.m., fasting is much more difficult!) Muslims see fasting as a way of becoming more compassionate, being in solidarity with human beings who do not have enough to eat. *Iftar*, which means "breaking the fast" in Arabic, is the evening meal during Ramadan and often occurs as a community meal at the mosque.

Christians most often fast during Lent, the forty days before Easter Sunday. When I was a child (the rules have since changed), Catholics also fasted and abstained from eating meat every Friday, a discipline many Catholics still follow. Now we abstain from eating meat on Ash Wednesday, which begins the season of Lent, and every Friday during Lent.

Jewish people refrain from eating and drinking (even water) on Yom Kippur (Day of Atonement). It is a complete, twenty-five-hour fast beginning before sunset on the evening before Yom Kippur and ending after nightfall on the day of Yom Kippur. There are also additional restrictions, such as not washing and bathing, not anointing one's body (with cosmetics, deodorants, and so on), not wearing leather shoes, and not engaging in sexual relations.

If you have never had an intentional experience of spiritual fasting, this is an area of prayer you might want to explore further. It is a discipline that can focus your prayers: When you are "empty," you can more easily open yourself to a deeper experience of the Holy.

I love the way this story makes the point:

A Cup of Tea

A young professor, wanting to learn from a spiritual master who lived in another country, contacted him and was invited to come and study during the summer break. The professor was thrilled. When he arrived at the master's home, he thanked the master for all the information in the master's books.

The master asked the professor if he wished to have a cup of tea.

As the master prepared the tea, the professor, hoping to impress the master, continued to speak of his studies. As the professor spoke, the master set out the cups and brewed the tea. Then the master began to pour—and kept on pouring long after the cup was full. The tea spilled on the table and onto the floor.

The professor yelled, "Stop! Can't you see the cup is full?"

"Yes, indeed, the cup is as full as is your mind. If you wish to study with me, you must empty yourself," replied the master.

You must empty yourself. Though the discipline of fasting may seem "out of step with the times … in a culture where the landscape is dotted with shrines to the Golden Arches and an assortment of Pizza Temples,"[2] setting aside and directing your hunger toward God may lead you to a feast of all that is sacred.

A Fasting Prayer Exercise

I believe that the fasting itself *is* prayer because it makes us more conscious than we usually are. Here is a simple fasting exercise that will help you understand what I mean.

First, choose a food you like, a food that, if it were missing from your diet, you would definitely notice its absence! Then choose a period of time (a day, a week, a month, whatever time frame you feel comfortable with) to go without this food. Every time you miss this food, let your awareness take you beyond yourself.

Here's an example: My two favorite food groups are butter and salt. During the season of Lent (the forty days before Easter Sunday), I stop eating both. Every time I sit down to a meal, I am aware of not eating salt or butter. It is then that I think of people who are in dire straights, people who do without daily, and not by choice. I become aware of my sisters and brothers of whom I am usually not conscious. I pray that my awareness may strengthen my resolve to share with those who have less. Fasting *becomes* my prayer.

Secret 3

Your Senses Are Vehicles of Prayer

We have to leap into faith through the senses.... I was drawn to the Church in my youth because it appealed to the senses. The music speaking to the ear, the incense to the sense of smell, the appeal of color to the eye, stained glass, ikons and statues, the bread and wine to the taste, the touch of rich vestments and altar linens, the touch of holy water, oils, the sign of the cross, the beating of the breast.

—*Dorothy Day,* The Catholic Worker

There is another secret of prayer within our bodies that we use every day: our senses. We're quite familiar with the forms of prayer that require discipline of the mind, but we don't usually tend to think of our senses as having anything to do with prayer. Yet each of our senses offers a unique connection to our source.

I like to think of our senses in the way Rabi'a of Basra, perhaps the most influential female saint in Islam, expresses it: There is nothing that happens in our life that does not give us the possibility of becoming more aware.

We have been given the gift of five senses: sight, hearing, smell, taste, and touch. Each of these senses has a corollary in the body: eyes, ears, nose, tongue, and skin. And with each part of our body, we have the possibility of becoming more aware of God, more connected with the Holy.

The Eyes Have It

Opening one's eyes may take a lifetime.

Seeing is done in a flash.

—*Anthony de Mello*

If someone were to ask you "How do you know God?," one of your first responses might be, "I read the Bible"—or the Qur'an, or the Torah, or whatever text your religion considers sacred. In cultures that are literate, using our eyes to read is probably the most common way we approach the Divine.

Most religious traditions have a sacred scripture they believe expresses God's thoughts: the Vedas of the Hindus, the Torah of the Jewish people, the Qur'an of the Muslims, the Pali Canon and Mahayana texts of Buddhism, the Christian New Testament, the Book of Mormon, the Tao Te Ching of Taoism, the Guru Granth Sahib of Sikhism, the writings of Swedenborg, the Avesta of Zoroastrianism, and many more. These sacred texts contain stories, poems, hymns, laws, customs, incantations, and rituals that help us understand the concept of mystery and the purpose of our lives.

Among Christians, there is a practice called *Lectio Divina* (Latin for "divine reading") that is a way of "praying" scripture. There are four parts to the exercise: reading the text consciously "as if for the first time"; reflecting, being attentive to what it says to you in your heart; opening your heart to respond to the message; and, finally, resting in the Holy and being with the deeper meaning of this scripture for you.

Christians are not the only ones who use reading as an entrée into the Holy. Although raised in Catholicism, Karen Armstrong writes in her autobiography, *The Spiral Staircase*, about her identification with the passion of Jews when she speaks of achieving ecstatic moments through study, often in the library. Jews celebrate Shavuot as the moment of receiving Torah from God on Mount Sinai, and one of the most beloved traditions of this feast is staying up all night studying and learning the text.

During the month of Ramadan, the holiest period in the Islamic year, Muslims read (or recite) a section of the Qur'an each evening after sharing the *iftar* (a meal that breaks the fast). The entire text is read within the month.

The spirituality of reading can be a means of intimacy with God, as Ursuline Sister Nancy Malone expresses so eloquently in her book *Walking a Literary Labyrinth*.

> For me, reading has been and is a spiritual practice. It is my partner in a conversation we are always having with ourselves (our interiority), influencing who I've thought I was, who I wanted to be, who I am and am called to be…. [I]t has been a midwife at rebirths I have undergone (conversions), and it has, at times, taught me lessons about who I am not. I have found a kind of intimacy—an exchange of selves—in reading, and have been helped by it toward an intimacy with myself and with God.[1]

If we are to consider all the ways in which we can use our sense of sight to connect with God, we also need to consider the spiritual practices that incorporate signs and symbols. A sign indicates the existence of something not immediately apparent. A symbol is a representation of something else, something invisible. Signs reach us in our *heads*. Symbols reach us in our *gut*. We *reflect* on signs, but we *respond* to symbols.

An experience I had as a campus minister at an academy for girls demonstrates the difference between the two terms. One of the most beloved teachers at the academy was confined to a wheelchair and was always accompanied by her service dog. When this teacher died of pneumonia, it was a traumatic event for faculty, staff, and students. The school's crisis management team met to discuss how best to heal our community and decided to place her empty wheelchair and her dog's bed at the front door of the school, surrounded by flowers, as symbols of our loss. A poster with pictures and facts about her life was also placed a short distance away from the symbols.

As students and faculty began to enter the building, the tears began to flow. The symbols gave us a place to grieve—but they also created a bit of a furor. Some of the faculty were not comfortable with these external manifestations of grief. The symbols of our dearly loved friend and teacher reached us in the gut, and we had to deal *viscerally* with her absence, while the poster had reminded us of our loss only *intellectually*. (Interestingly, no one had a problem with the poster.)

Signs and symbols are found in every religious tradition and can have different meanings for different people. A cross, for example, on a chain around someone's neck is usually a sign that the person is Christian, while a burning cross is a symbol of hatred. A Star of David on a chain is probably a sign of a person's Jewish heritage, while a Star of David sewn onto a coat is a symbol of the Holocaust.

In most religious traditions, the language of sacred scriptures is symbolic, veiled, and subtle. Jews keep the scrolls in an ark; Muslims honor the Qur'an and would never put anything on top of the text or turn their backs to this holy book. The Bible (which contains both Jewish and Christian scriptures) is used in U.S. courts when someone takes an oath.

Every religion uses visual images to help us connect with the Holy. In Tibetan Buddhism, for example, all religious art is considered "support" for the spiritual journey. Mandalas (Sanskrit for "circle" or "completion") are especially valued. The circular shape of mandalas draws the attention of the eyes toward its center.

Sand mandalas are painstakingly created out of grains of colored sand by monks, and more recently by nuns. I once had the pleasure of meeting the nuns from Keydong Thuk-Che-Cho-Ling in Kathmandu, Nepal, who had come to Brandeis University to create a sand mandala. It took them two weeks to create this masterpiece. When they finished, they asked the Dalai Lama, who was visiting Brandeis at the same time, to ritualize the destruction of the mandala. A sand mandala is meant to be destroyed almost as soon as it is created, either by passing one's hands through the sand or using a small brush. Then the multicolored sand is collected and poured into a flowing body of water to illustrate that nothing is permanent and that everything returns to the earth.

Though the mandala is of Hindu or Buddhist origin, the concept of concentrating on something visual during meditation is common to many religious traditions. An example of a Christian mandala can be found in Gothic churches in circular windows filled with multicolored stained glass. These windows, called "rose windows," suggest a rose and its petals. Perhaps the best known of these windows is found in the Cathedral of Notre Dame in Paris.

Some traditions use icons (the Greek word for "images") as a
visual point of focus to support prayer or meditation. Specifically,
icons are paintings sacred to Greek, Russian, and Arabic Orthodox
Christianity. They are characterized by vibrant colors and often
gold-colored backgrounds. The figures portrayed are often intentionally elongated for symbolic reasons. For example, Jesus is often
portrayed with large ears and a small mouth, signifying his ability to
hear everything yet speak only wisdom. For Orthodox Christians,
these sacred paintings, along with frescoes and mosaics, are windows into heaven. In speaking of the need for icons, St. Theodore the
Studite wrote, "If contemplation with the intellect had been sufficient,
it would have sufficed for the Word to come among us intellectually
only."

Just as the term *mandala* is now used to refer to many symmetri-
cal geometric shapes, the term *icon* has come to mean more than styl-
ized paintings. Icons can be pictures of gurus in a Hindu temple,
statues of saints in Catholic churches and in Buddhist temples, meno-
rahs in Jewish homes, tikis of the South Pacific indigenous religions,
totems of Native Americans, crosses worn by Protestants, and, I would
add, pictures of the Kaaba in Mecca. Whatever form they take, these
images of the Holy are meant to be stared at. By staring, I mean truly
gazing at something long enough so that our eyes ultimately intuit the
presence of the Holy among us. And in that act of seeing, our eyes become vehicles for prayer.

Any visual reminder of the Divine in our world can be a sign or
symbol that opens our sight to this invisible presence. It can be a beautiful painting, a sunset, or a view at the top of a mountain. It can be
something as simple as the color of an exquisite rose or the mesmeriz-
ing drift of falling snow. Whenever we truly *see* something and, as in

the practice of *Lectio Divina*, stop to reflect, respond, and rest in the Holy, our seeing becomes prayer.

A "Seeing" Prayer Exercise

As a child, did you ever lie on your back gazing at the clouds overhead and try to "see" animals or people in the formations? Or did you ever lie on your stomach and study the miniature world of ants, especially when they were crawling in a line and carrying food? That is the kind of "seeing" that I am talking about when I say "praying with your eyes": being completely caught up in the world, totally present to the moment—no future, no past, just the now.

Try this simple exercise of seeing prayer. Go to a beautiful place in nature and find a comfortable place to sit or lie. Breathe deeply and look at the gift of your surroundings. Let your eyes feast on the wonders you behold. As you pray with your eyes, give yourself over to the moment.

Good Vibrations

Prayer is a groan.

—*St. Jerome*

In its simplest form, prayer is talking with the Holy. When we think of "talking," however, we usually think of some well-formed, coherent thoughts put into sentences. One of the secrets of prayer lies in discovering the power of the *sound* of a word.

Physicists—particularly those who study quantum mechanics—have learned from their research that everything is vibrating, everything that exists is eternally moving. Not just life forms such as animals and trees, but also stones and minerals and water. And, of course, us! Everything that exists, even human-made items, vibrates, and everything that vibrates creates sound.

The corollary is that some vibrations have a positive effect on us, and some have a negative effect. In his research on vibration in water, Dr. Masaru Emoto, director of the Hado Institute in Tokyo, has made some telling discoveries. He began his work by taking samples of both pure and polluted water and freezing them. He then photographed the frozen crystals and discovered that pure water formed beautiful crystals, while the crystals from the polluted water were malformed. Eventually, this led him to wonder how our words, the vibration of our spoken and written expressions, might affect crystal formation. He printed some words and attached them to containers of water. When the water froze, he once again photographed the crystal formations. Astoundingly, the crystals were influenced by the words on the container! Positive words, such as *love* or *gratitude,* created beautifully formed crystals. Negative words, such as *hate,* produced malformed crystals. The conclusion Emoto drew is that the words we choose have a power of their own that influences *everything* in our environment.

Stop for a moment to think about the implications of this when one word is repeated over and over again. In Eastern religions, these repeated words or phrases are called mantras. They are something akin to white noise and are used in meditation to silence the wandering conversations in our minds. Religious scholar Huston Smith says, "Mantras convert noise into sound and distracting chatter into holy formulas."

These "holy formulas" can be found in most religious traditions. Hindus chant the sound *Om*, which is considered to be the primordial sound of the universe, a groan of pleasure or pain, or a sound of comfort for an infant. Om includes three syllables and is pronounced "aah-ooo-mmm." The syllable *aah* stands for the creator Brahma, *ooo* the preserver Vishnu, and *mmm* the destroyer Shiva.

A Buddhist might use the mantra Om, meaning "spirit" or "Word of God." A Tibetan Buddhist might say, *"Om mani padme hum,"* meaning "O, thou jewel in the Lotus, hail." A Jewish person might use *Ribbono shel olam,* referring to God as "Creator of the universe." Christians might use Abba, the intimate Aramaic term for "father," which Jesus used to address God. Or the name *Jesus* or the word *peace.* Orthodox Christians use variations of what is called the Jesus prayer: "Lord Jesus Christ, Son of God, have mercy on me, a sinner."

The repetition of a mantra (sometimes by a group chanting together) eventually stills the mind, awakens the spirit, and opens the heart. It is a way of reaching for the Holy through sound. Any of us can create a mantra simply by repeating a word or phrase we deem sacred. Choosing the mantra is the easy part. The difficulty is in turning the mantra into a "ceaseless prayer" and incorporating it into our daily routine.

Benedictine nun Mary Margaret Funk writes in *Thoughts Matter: The Practice of the Spiritual Life*: "Ceaseless prayer is to continuously breathe the Jesus prayer or another prayer so that the prayer acts like a mantra always working on one's consciousness at a deeper level for the sake of union with God. In learning it, the first phase is mechanical, the second mental, and the third is mystical."[2]

In addition to the spoken word, sound vibrations can play an important role in prayer through music. Augustine of Hippo is often quoted as saying, "Those who sing, pray twice." Most religious traditions use both instrumental and vocal music for the purpose of praising God and expressing joy. When people gather together to sing, they create an energy that transforms their emotional life by consoling, affirming, and raising their spirits—sometimes to the point of ecstasy.

I was fortunate to grow up on Gregorian chant. In Catholic elementary school, we were taught how to read the square notes, and we sang every Sunday at the children's Mass in the basement of the church. For me, the tones elicited an automatic movement toward a meditative state. The candle-lit lower church, the smell of beeswax, the incense, the monotony of tones—even my incomprehension of the Latin—created a soothing, reflective space that transcended my child's world and brought me into a place of holiness that I did not have the words or the understanding to explain. But it was a powerful experience, and I believe it was prayer.

One of the beautiful aspects of praying with sound is that it makes prayer accessible to everyone, even if all we can do is groan. As the words of the Christian New Testament reminds, "[The] Spirit intercedes with sighs too deep for words" (Romans 8:26).

A "Sound" Prayer Exercise

If you have never prayed using a mantra, give yourself a chance to experiment with it. Choose a word that has a sacred connection for you. Set aside time (ideally, twenty minutes) at the beginning of your day to meditate on your word. Say the word aloud to begin with and then repeat it silently. During the day, whenever you find yourself doing something mindless, such as waiting in traffic, bring the word to consciousness over and over again. Let your mantra become ceaseless prayer.

If this form of wordless prayer is a familiar practice for you, then try using a simple sound, such as Om, or whatever sound or sigh you are comfortable with. Repeat your sound as you send it to God.

Hear Ye, Hear Ye

The value of consistent prayer is not that [God]
will hear us, but that we will hear God.
            —*Rev. William McGill*

Dr. George Washington Carver of Tuskegee Institute (now University)
was superbly aware of sound vibrations. When asked how he could
perform healing miracles on ailing plants, Carver replied, "All flowers
talk to me and so do hundreds of little living things in the woods. I
learn what I know by watching and loving everything…. The secrets
are in the plants."[3]

Perhaps most of us are not as in tune with nature as Dr. Carver
was, but if we can hear, we have access to another secret of prayer:
hearing the Holy in the vibrations of sound.

As a child attending a Catholic elementary school, I was taught
to be conscious of bells. Of course, there were school bells, which the
sisters rang at the beginning of the day so that we could assemble, and
there were little bells that denoted a change of class subject. More
striking were the noon bells that would stop everyone in the school-
yard, and we would say a prayer called the "Angelus" (picture Jean-
François Millet's painting *The Angelus*). (The bells also rang at 6 a.m.
and 6 p.m., but we were not in the care of the sisters at those times, so
we did not have to pay attention.)

Archaeological evidence of the use of bells is overwhelming: Spec-
imens of bells used in ancient Babylonia and in Egypt, as well as by the
Romans and Greeks, are still preserved. We know that primitive Celtic
people attached an extraordinary importance to bells. A very large
number of these ancient bells, more than sixty, are still in existence. The
first Christian writer who frequently spoke of bells (*signa*) was Gregory

of Tours (ca. 585). It appears that they were rung before church services and to rouse the monks from their beds. In many churches across
the English countryside today, the ringing of the bells is a solemn tradition that began in the early part of the seventeenth century. "Change
ringing," as it is called, is a process of ringing a series of mathematical
patterns without attempting to play a conventional tune.

The custom in convents used to be that clocks would chime the
hours. The eldest sister in the room would then say, "Sisters, please let
us remember the Holy Presence of God." And all those present would
attend to the presence of the Divine in their midst.

Although there are no bells in Islam, Muslims use the human
voice for the call to prayer (*Adhan*) five times a day. Fifteen to twenty
minutes before prayer time, the muezzin climbs the minaret and calls
out the *Adhan* in a rhythmic way:

> *God is Great.*
> *I bear witness that there is no god except the One God.*
> *I bear witness that Muhammad is the messenger of God.*
> *Hurry to prayer.*
> *Hurry to success.*
> *God is Great.*
> *There is no god except the One God.*
> *Prayer is better than sleep.*

The call gives worshipers time for cleansing before they settle into
the mosque. Then a second call, the *Iquma* (or *Iqumah*), is given to denote that prayer is beginning.

Although you may not be near the sound of bells, the point is that
any vibration of sound has the potential to call us to God, even every-

day sounds such as the telephone ringing! In Plum Village and the other monasteries developed by Buddhist peace activist and monk Thich Nhat Hanh, one of the important practices is that of "bells of mindfulness." When a bell is sounded, people stop talking and moving, relax their bodies, and become aware of their breathing. But it doesn't stop there. Retreatants are taught that they can use the ringing of the phone, the cry of a baby—even the sound of fire engines and ambulances!—as bells of mindfulness.

Whatever sounds are present in your daily life, when you pay particular attention to them, in a mindful way, you have another opportunity to connect with the source of life.

A "Listening" Prayer Exercise

Give yourself an experience of listening prayer. Find a place where you can be still and begin to let yourself be aware of all the sounds around you. Start with the sounds that seem furthest away and name what you hear. Thank your Creator for that sound and listen for what God might be saying to you in the sound. Continue listening, naming, and reflecting on different sounds, each progressively closer to you, until you get to your body. Conclude with listening to the sounds of your body—your breathing, your heartbeat—and end with a prayer of gratitude.

Smells and Bells

The sense of smell is the sense of imagination.

—*Jean Jacques Rousseau*

All our senses have incredible abilities to pick up information about our surroundings, but our sense of smell is unique. While other senses, such as taste and touch, send messages to the brain via a circuitous route, our sense of smell is the only sense that has a direct connection to the limbic brain, where emotional memories are processed. Therefore, we have a strong emotional response to smells, and they have the power to elicit both memory and arousal. A certain fragrance can immediately remind us of a specific experience, even if it was in the distant past. As Helen Keller so accurately stated, "Smell is a potent wizard that transports you across thousands of miles and all the years you have lived."

Mary Hunt, codirector of Women's Alliance for Theology, Ethics and Ritual (WATER), often speaks of the "smells and bells" of Catholic ritual. I know what she means. I grew up in a pre–Vatican II world where the ritual language in the Catholic Church was Latin, real candles were multitudinous, bells were rung inside and outside the church, incense permeated the ceremonies, and the priest wore ornately designed vestments. We were not sensory-deprived. To this day, the smell of beeswax and certain types of incense takes me right back to that experience of my youth.

Throughout the Bible there are many references to incense as a symbol of prayer rising to God. Jehovah's instructions to Moses in the Book of Exodus are filled with fire, burnt offerings, and incense, even giving a specific formula for creating incense:

> Take sweet spices, stacte, and onycha, and galbanum, sweet spices with pure frankincense (an equal part of each), and make an incense blended as by the perfumer, seasoned with salt, pure and holy; and you shall beat some of it into powder, and put part of it before the covenant in the tent of meeting where I shall meet with you; it shall be for you most holy. (Exodus 30:34–36)

Within Jewish mysticism, Kabbalah, each stage of breathing is understood to relate to one of the senses. The first stage—inhaling—corresponds to the sense of smell. When we inhale, we smell the air, and this is considered the most spiritual of the senses.

Native Americans burn grasses and herbs to cleanse an area in a ritual known as smudging. Cedar, sweet grasses, or sage are bound together and then dried to make a thick stick that will smoke rather than burn. The smoking stick or smudge stick is carried throughout a room, with particular attention paid to corners and difficult-to-reach areas. Or, using a large feather, the smoke is brushed around whatever needs to be cleansed or wherever negative energy needs to be cleared. In theory, the smoke attaches itself to negative energy, and as the smoke clears, it takes the negative energy with it, releasing it into another space where it will be regenerated into positive energy.

Lighting a fragrant candle or using incense can move our whole being into readiness and a heightened state of spiritual awareness. Every time I sit down to write, I light a candle. (I'm particularly fond of pure beeswax candles because they leave a lovely scent of honey and don't drip.) Every time I smell the candle burning, I know what I am to do. I also use a fragrant candle to meditate. My nose reminds me that, just as the fragrance is invisible but very present, so too the Holy is unseen but very much with me.

A "Fragrance" Prayer Exercise

Using a fragrance as a means of prayer can be a very powerful experience. To sample this vehicle of praying, select a scented candle or some incense. Set it in a clear space in a room and sit quietly for a moment, reflecting on this quotation from the Christian scriptures or a similar thought from your tradition:

> And the smoke of the incense, with the prayers of the saints, rose before God. (Revelation 8:4)
>
> Then light your candle or incense. Begin to name your thoughts and feelings and concerns, letting each one rise up to God with the flame or the smoke. Sense that your prayers are joining with "the prayers of the saints." Close by repeating this phrase from the Psalms:
>
> Let my prayer rise before you like incense
> And my hands like an evening offering. (Psalm 141:2)

Taste and See

Taste and see that God is good.
—*Psalm 34:8* (The Scottish Psalter)

I know many women who, when given a piece of really good chocolate, exclaim prayerfully, "Oh, my God!" A pagan friend of mine calls chocolate "the food of the Goddess"! Maybe the taste that makes you swoon is something with depth, such as a particular coffee, or something with a unique texture, such as crème brûlée. Whenever you truly savor the taste of something, it is an experience that goes beyond simply eating.

Eating is something we do every day, but we're often more engaged in the *activity* of eating—talking with others or hurrying to get on to more important things—than in the *awareness* of eating. Buddhists encourage a practice called "mindful eating" that shifts the focus from receiving nourishment and satisfying hunger to being aware and appreciative, and this becomes a form of prayer.

Many religious traditions link special foods with sacred rituals to make them more meaningful. When Muslims break their fast at Ramadan, they do so in the same way the Prophet did—by eating a date. When my friend Sepi invited me to an *iftar*, the breaking of the fast, at her mosque, I decided to join her that day in the fast. I was very aware of my hunger when I arrived at the mosque. After the greetings and blessings, a dish of dates was passed around. Eating that date not only broke my hunger but also became a prayer for me.

I come from a tradition where the most sacred ritual involves eating bread and drinking wine. This ritual recalls the activities and words Jesus shared with his followers during the Seder meal that was his last supper before his crucifixion. During the Seder meal, which takes place on the first two nights of Passover, ritual food symbolizing the story of Moses leading the Israelites out of slavery into the Promised Land is placed on a special Seder plate in the center of the table. As the Passover story is read aloud, eating these foods accompanies the listening. Whenever I attend a Seder, I am always struck by the taste of the foods on the Seder plate: bitter herbs, horseradish, *choroset* (a combination of walnuts, apples, cinnamon, and sweet red wine), parsley dipped in salt water, the matzah (dry, crackerlike unleavened bread). Each taste is a reminder of some aspect of the Passover story. The very eating from the Seder plate becomes a prayer and a reminder of a greater reality.

Perhaps you have a favorite meal that reminds you of a special time or person in your life. In my family, my sister remembers our ancestors every Thanksgiving as she prepares the meal exactly as my grandmother and grandaunts did. She serves the meal on the china and silverware that she inherited from them. A meal can become a memorial in itself! When my sister-in-law died, my brother and I ate at her favorite restaurant and ordered her favorite dishes.

Ritualizing a memory, feeding and sharing with others, and eating mindfully can all become forms of prayer.

A "Tasting" Prayer Exercise

Vietnamese Buddhist monk Thich Nhat Hanh speaks of a beautiful prayer with an orange. Although this exercise involves all the senses, the completion of it is taste. Choose an orange and sit quietly with it in your hands. Imagine where it came from and how it arrived into your hands. Thank the Creator, the grower, the fruit picker, the truck driver, and the grocery worker who made it possible for you to have such a gift. Feel the texture of the skin. Begin to peel the deep orange skin and be aware of the aroma of the oil that escapes. Notice how the fruit is enclosed in yet another protective membrane. Peel a section and bite into it. Let the aroma fill your nostrils and let the juice melt over your tongue. Taste and see the goodness of nature.

Reach Out and Touch

They're all grand—hearing and smell and sight and taste, but touch—touch is elemental. There's no kidding about touch; touch is a biological necessity without which the body as well as the soul falters.

—*Sherry Cohen,* The Magic of Touch

Usually, if one of our senses is impaired in some way, the other senses increase their sensitivity and become more powerful, attempting to compensate for the missing sense. The truth is, we can survive the loss of our sight, our hearing, our sense of smell, and even our sense of taste, but we cannot live without touch.

Touch can be either sensual or sexual. Sensual touch is safe, comforting, and healing and is literally a daily need in our lives. We use sensual touch to communicate care and calm to another. In contrast, sexual touch puts a person on edge. It is not done to calm someone, but rather to arouse. This differentiation is of utmost importance to those of us who live in a culture where all touch is considered sexual, where all touch is suspect.

Touch may well be the sense that most people are afraid to use in their faith. There is a widespread concern that somehow touch equals sex, and that sex and holiness do not belong in the same room. So let's begin there. For starters, sex is what keeps life going. Because it is so basic to life, I believe our sexual energy plays an important part in our prayer, our meditation, and our contemplation. In fact, I would go so far as to say that contemplation is related to our sexual capacity for joy. Italian sculptor Gianlorenzo Bernini knew this when he carved the Ecstasy of St. Teresa (Ávila), and so obviously did Teresa, as she wrote in her autobiography:

> Beside me on the left appeared an angel in bodily form.... He was not tall but short, and very beautiful; and his face was so aflame that he appeared to be one of the highest ranks of angels, who seem to be all on fire.... In his hands I saw a great golden spear, and at the iron tip there appeared to be a point of fire. This he plunged into my heart several times so that it penetrated my entrails. When he pulled it out I felt that he took them with it, and left me utterly consumed by the great love of God. The pain was so severe that it made me utter several moans. The sweetness caused by this intense pain is so extreme that one cannot possibly wish it to cease, nor is one's soul content with anything but God.

This is not a physical but a spiritual pain, though the body has some share in it—even a considerable share.[4]

The biblical Song of Songs is certainly an affirmation of the joy of sexuality. Perhaps the most infamous and least understood tradition that embraces the body in its entirety is Tantric Buddhism of Tibet. The Tantric Buddhist believes that one can attain union with the Divine through the body through extremely disciplined sexual practices. The Western world, particularly with its preoccupation with sex, has taken many of these teachings out of context and has left us confused about how to assuage the human need to be touched, while being acutely aware of how touch can be abused.

But in its purest form, sexual touch is a means of reaching beyond what we can understand or explain to something transcendent. I've thought for a number of years now that the vow of chastity is a vow to use one's sexual energy to go to God. In any number of ways, our sexual energy puts us in touch with our Creator.

There are many other ways in which the sense of touch can be integral to prayer. It may surprise you to learn that two-thirds of the world's population uses touch during prayer, in the form of prayer beads. Wearing and using beads are tactile ways of communicating with the source of our being. Whether the beads are made of bone, seeds, stone, shells, wood, olive pits, or even crushed rose petals, they can support us in our quest for the Divine.

Beads used for religious purposes are found on every inhabited continent. Probably the first were just pebbles or shells moved from one side to another in a counting process. Anyone familiar with the African game *mankala* knows the seemingly simple yet profoundly challenging concept of moving stones from one place to another. The

Matabele of central Africa had beads that were known as "ambassador beads," for they were used to elicit goodwill from the Divine. For the Yoruba of West Africa, beads can represent the Divine itself.

The earliest written documentation of the use of beads for religious purposes comes from the Egyptians in North Africa. But the Hindu tradition, with beads called *mala* (which means "rose" or "garland" in Sanskrit), is probably the oldest. It wasn't until the twelfth century that Christians adopted rosaries as a means for both vocal and silent (or mental) prayer.

Rosaries, or stringed prayer beads, function in a variety of ways. They can be cataphatic, as in the Roman Catholic tradition in which we remember different events in the life of Jesus. Or they can be apophatic, when words dissolve and bring us to "no thing" or to emptiness. Beads or rosaries can help focus our attention and aid our concentration when we "say the bead" or use them as a means of counting, if we believe that saying a certain number of prayers is important.

Buddhists, for example, chant with a string of 108 beads. There are also 108 beads in a Hindu *mala*. Greek Orthodox Christian rosaries, called *kombologion*, or "string of knots," consist of a woolen rope with 33, 50, or 100 knots. Some Orthodox bead strings are called *metanoia*, meaning "a change of mind"—which, of course, is the whole point. Russian Orthodox rosaries are called *chotki* and number 33, 100, or even 300. Roman Catholics use 59 beads and a crucifix. Anglican Catholics have renewed their interest in rosaries, and since the 1980s use a strand of 33 prayer beads.

Of great interest to me are the beads used by Armenian pilgrims when they make a haj to Jerusalem. This rosary is composed of 14 smooth, flat, rectangular semiprecious stones strung on two strings.

At each stop along the *Via Dolorosa* (the Sorrowful Way, or the Stations of the Cross), the pilgrims touch a stone to remember Jesus's walk to his crucifixion.

Muslims use beads known as *tasbih*. There are 99 beads, and each one stands for a name, or rather an attribute, of the Holy One. (The hundredth name, the Name of the Essence, is found only in Heaven.) My friend Najwa gave me my first *tasbih* many years ago. When I use the *tasbih*, I know that if I am present to each bead, it will take me twenty minutes or so to pray the 99 beads. As I touch each bead, rather than reciting the names of God as Muslims do, I breathe. This is essentially a practice of Being Here Now, which is a teaching in nearly every spiritual tradition. I like to use my friend Sondra's approach: "Each bead is like a new day, a new awakening."

Jewish people do not use beads, but experience tactile prayer in another way. Some Jewish people pray three times a day with the tefillin, two small leather boxes containing sacred scripture. The boxes are attached to long leather straps, which the pray-ers wrap in a specific pattern around their forehead and arm.

Whether you use beads or a rosary or a *tasbih* or tefillin—or even something as simple as stones from the beach or your garden—objects can be tactile reminders to be more "in touch" with the Divine.

A "Touching" Prayer Exercise

Give yourself an opportunity to experience prayer as touch. Find a stone that feels good in your hand and sit quietly with it for a few minutes, feeling its weight, its shape, its unique texture. Is it rough or smooth? Cold or warm? Round or asymmetrical? (It might help increase your sensitivity to touch if you close your eyes.) Consider the stone's history: how long it was in the process of being formed, where it found its home in the world. Then think of the stone as something that is part of God's creation, something the world would not be complete without. Give thanks to the Creator for the complexities of the universe—including you!

Secret 4

Diversity Nourishes Prayer

Just as our bodies need nourishment,
so too, our souls, which hunger for
God, need to be nourished by prayer.
—*Poor Clares Galway*

Eating is a basic human activity. If we don't eat, we die! It is the same in our spiritual life: If we don't pray, we starve spiritually. We need prayer to nourish our souls.

But consider the reverse for a moment: Is it possible that we need to nourish prayer before it can nourish us?

Think of the difference between a bland diet and a series of gourmet dinners. If we eat plain bread and tasteless soup over and over again, we may be taking the edge off our hunger, but we are not satisfying our need for nourishment, let alone our need for variety. Not only our stomachs but also our taste buds will be crying out for a change!

It is the same with prayer: If we repeat the same words one hundred times, without being present and mindful, it offers us no nourishment for spiritual growth.

Ponder for a moment the idea of prayer as eating. It takes a little creativity, perhaps even a few cooking lessons, and certainly a willingness to experiment with different foods to awaken our palette. So, too, on the spiritual front: The secret to developing our prayer life is to nourish our prayers with a bit of diversity.

The Principle of Differentiation

Diversity is no longer something that we tolerate.
It is something that we esteem as a necessary condition for a livable universe.

—*Thomas Berry*

We humans are a diverse lot in every respect. We love a huge variety of color, from our gardens to our clothes, from our décor to our cars and phones and appliances. When it comes to climate, some people like it hot, some like it cold. The same thing applies to food: Some like it hot, some like it cold.

Having lived for many years in African American communities in the Midwest and in the South, I am blessed to have acquired a taste for collard greens, pot likker (the juice from cooked greens), corn bread, any type of barbeque, catfish, fried chicken, biscuits, black-eyed peas, and grits. When I first saw collards growing in a weed-free garden carefully tended by a couple in their nineties, I asked what those tall stalks with big green leaves were. The elderly woman replied, "Collards." When I explained that I had never seen collards before, she looked at me with wonder and asked, "Well, child, what *do* you eat?"

Truth and Perception

As the elephant passed, four blind men extended their hands. The first one felt the trunk and cried, "The elephant is just like a huge snake." The second man felt the leg and cried, "No way. The elephant is more like a huge tree." The third man felt the elephant's big body and cried, "No, it is more like a building." The fourth man seized hold of the tail, and yelled. "No, no, no. You are all wrong. The elephant is like a whip."

This classic story reminds us that no one person knows the whole of the Holy. If our minds are "made up," or are already full of what we think we know, there is no room for additional wisdom. If we believe that we know all there is to know of the Divine through our tradition, we may think we are full—even satisfied—until we realize how much we don't know. When we open ourselves to other spiritual traditions, we become hungry for more knowledge, and this hunger reactivates our willingness and desire to learn. Just as our physical hunger seeks variety—sometimes we crave something salty, other times, something sweet—so too does our spiritual hunger seek variety to feel satisfied.

A Diversity Prayer Exercise

Choose a faith tradition you don't know much about. Find out what you can about it: Look at books, check the Internet, visit that faith's place of worship. Be especially on the alert for prayers from this tradition. Select one prayer that you can ponder to see what it says to you and what it tells you about the Holy One.

Stories Fuel Prayer

Stories are the creative conversion of life itself into a
more powerful, clearer, more meaningful experience.
They are the currency of human contact.

—*Robert McKee*

Stories are often a nonthreatening way to sample difference: We can
open and close books at will, and books do not talk back. Stories can
crack open a door to a world that exists and yet is not easily seen; stories can teach us about the invisible. Trust, openness, love, courage,
and kindness do not have an address; they cannot be picked up on our
way home at the grocery store. Yet we need them, and stories can lead
us to the places where we can find them, places beyond our familiar
sacred stories and traditions.

Stories are found in every religious tradition, and many compile
their stories in their sacred scriptures. The Hindu Panchatantra stories
began as a way of illustrating, through a series of animal tales, how
young men might be trained to succeed the throne. The Buddha
adopted these tales, called Jataka stories, to explain core concepts and
to emphasize important moral values. Jewish midrash is a method of
fleshing out the stories of the Bible by imagining what might have happened or been said between the lines—"searching out the fullness," as
Charles T. Davis, professor emeriti of religion at Appalachian State
University, articulates. Jesus was a consummate storyteller and used
parables to explain his teachings. Christians in the Middle Ages created morality plays and allegories to explain their beliefs to people
who could not read. Hadiths of Islam, stories of the way of life of the
Prophet Muhammad, help Muslims discover what to imitate and what
to avoid.

No matter what form a story takes, it can be like a nut that has been handed to us: The teaching is the meat inside the nut, but we can discover it only when we are hungry enough to crack the shell. I am reminded of the theology teacher who taught in parables and stories. The students listened with both delight and disappointment, sometimes feeling that they were not getting the "meat" of the teachings. When they complained, the teacher would reply, "My dears, the shortest distance between you and Truth is a story."

When we cannot physically come into contact with another tradition, we can look to books, both fictional and nonfictional, for the meat of the Truth—*if* we are willing to look beyond what we "know." There is a story taken from the Sufi tradition that beautifully and succinctly illustrates how our spirits can be nourished when we are open to hearing a different voice. A pilgrim asks a Sufi master if the Qu'ran is a good book to read. The Sufi master replies, "You should ask yourself if you are in a state to profit by it."

Stories prime our hearts and minds to seek the Divine and open us to hear the Divine Voice in a new way—which is especially valuable on the days when we hear only our own voice! Listening to a sacred story can be a meditation. Telling a sacred story can be a prayer. Being with a sacred story can lead us to contemplation of the Divine.

When I was in the novitiate, I studied theology at St. Louis University's Divinity School. One of my favorite professors, John Walsh, SJ, taught a course called "God and Man in Cinema." He told us that he would sit in a theater until he "got" the movie. He would see it over and over until he could explain what the artist was saying.

I see stories in the same light, whether they be stories of Teresa of Ávila's conversations with God, tales from Reb Moshe Waldoks's *The Big Book of Jewish Humor*, the account of Tibetan Buddhist nun

Tenzin Palmo's twelve years in a cave, or Paul Reps's stories from Zen. Perhaps more than any other tool, stories from a variety of traditions help me see the breadth of the Divine in my life and inspire my prayer life. I savor them, ponder them, much like something I tuck in my pocket and carry with me throughout the day. They touch my soul and live in my heart. They are at my beck and call as I contemplate the Holy in my life.

In this way, stories become prayers for me, guiding me to live more compassionately, more thoughtfully, more aware of possibility. They prod my imagination and curiosity, incite my desire to dig for the deeper meaning of everyday events, and stir me to marvel at the breadth of the Holy in action.

I have been touched by stories for as long as I can remember, from the tales my grandfather told me about "the old country," to the adventures Aunt Catherine related about life on Bunker Hill in Charlestown, to the Grimms' fairy tales that my mother would read to us as we cuddled on the couch in the den. One of my greatest joys was learning to read and then being able to pick out my own storybooks from the library.

I've always had a particular liking for stories that have several layers of meaning. The first such tale I ever read by myself was Aesop's fable of the Sun and the North Wind's attempt to change behavior.

The Sun and the North Wind

The Sun and the North Wind each tried to make a man take off his cloak. The North Wind blew and blew, but the man got colder and colder as he hugged the cloak tighter to his body. Then it was the Sun's turn. The Sun shone brightly, and the man removed his cloak.

Even as a child, I "got" it. I understood that it was a story illustrating how showering warmth is a more successful approach to changing a person's behavior than is cold, demanding force.

Aesop's fables are fun ways to learn how to be human! Perhaps you remember this one:

The Goose That Laid a Golden Egg

A man had a goose that laid eggs of gold. But as the man grew rich, he grew greedy. Thinking to get at once all the gold the goose could give, he killed the goose. But when he opened it, he found nothing.

Stories like this remind us of who we are and who we need to become. They are time-tested traditions that convey wisdom about how to live. They can solidify beliefs, explain natural phenomena, offer models of behavior, and give warnings. Stories are flexible; they flow from life, and as they are passed on, they help us adapt to new situations.

Stories can also expand our thoughts about how we can align ourselves with the Holy, as the following story drawn from the Jewish tradition illustrates:

The Woods

There once was a small village. And in that village lived a man, Moshe, and a rabbi. Each morning the man would wake up, make breakfast, wash himself, and prepare to go out. And each morning he would leave his humble home and head into the woods that could be found on the edge of the village. He wandered for hours in those woods, never seeing another soul, and only returned in time to go to work.

The rabbi started to take notice of Moshe. After about two weeks, the rabbi decided one evening to go to Moshe's home and ask him about his daily adventures. Moshe welcomed the rabbi in and made some tea. They entered into conversation, and right before the rabbi was about to take his leave, he said to Moshe, "I have noticed that each day you walk into the woods. I wonder why do you go there?"

Moshe responded by telling the rabbi that he went to the woods to find God, to pray.

The rabbi replied gently, "That is a very good thing. I am glad that you are searching for God, but don't you know that God is the same everywhere?"

Now Moshe looked at the rabbi and smiled, "Yes, but I am not."

When you finish reading this book, not all the material will stay with you. However, it's likely that you will remember some of the stories. That's the reason so many faith traditions choose stories as the vehicle to convey wisdom teachings: They are easy to remember. Even if you don't understand the story, it will sit with you until the day its meaning breaks through, until the day you crack the shell.

The next time your prayers seem empty, listen to a story. Read a tale. Fill up on some "soul food" that will move you to continue seeking the sacred in your life. And know that you are in prayer.

A Story Prayer Exercise

Think of a story from your childhood. (You may want to look at a children's story collection to jog your memory.) Revisit the story with an "empty" approach—not as if you already know all the layers of meaning in the story. Listen for what the Divine Voice might be saying to you. Let your thoughts, as you ponder the story, become your prayer.

The "Spice" of Other People's Prayers

As food is necessary for the body,
prayer is necessary for the soul.
—*Mahatma Gandhi*

Eating is something we need to do day in, day out. But sometimes it gets to be a chore just to think of what to fix for the next meal. We get tired of eating the same things over and over again. Sometimes we think how marvelous it would be if we had a personal chef to prepare a gourmet meal for us! But even if we had *that* same meal every day, no matter how good it was, we would soon tire of it.

Savoring the prayers of other people and religious traditions—especially those who have been on the spiritual path longer than we have—is a wonderful way to "spice up" our spiritual diet. Other people's prayers can open our taste buds beyond our familiar prayers to new flavors that renew our spiritual energy.

I like to collect prayers that stir me, touch me. Granted, some prayer books are boring. But as my friend Ellen told me when she was studying church law, "There is so much manure here, there has got to be a pony somewhere." Well, I have found a lot of ponies, and small as they are, I ride them.

The buffet of prayer options offers unlimited choices; I offer some of the prayers that have stirred me. Several are ancient, practiced, traditional; some are funny, insightful, awesome, and challenging. Their concepts come from traditions that are Hindu, Buddhist,

Jewish, Muslim, Christian, humanitarian, and agnostic. I borrow or adapt or adopt them. I read, sing, memorize, say, share, and pray them. Some are treasures that I hide in my bedside drawer, encircled with an elastic band. A few live in my memory where I can draw them up on a moment's notice. Some are stuffed in a gigantic folder in my file cabinet. Many of them are typed, or handwritten, or scissored out of unsuspecting texts; a few have been gifts from seekers. The Internet even coughs them up now and then, if you know where to look.

The following are prayers I use daily, weekly, or monthly. I hope you find them as nourishing as I do. I encourage you to begin collecting prayers that touch you. Look for prayers that are funny or poignant or consciousness-raisers. Prayers that you can say every day. Prayers that you can frame or post on your desk or keep in a folder. Prayers that you can reach for in time of need.

In other words, prayers that are soul food.

A Prayer of Reassurance

The first "Protestant prayer" I learned was Psalm 23; I have always been reassured by the words, which are so very pastoral. There is something about the King James Version that rolls beautifully off the tongue, so I have adapted it to fit my ever-evolving feminist consciousness.

> *You are my shepherd, I shall not want,*
> *You maketh me to lie down in green pastures;*
> *You leadeth me beside still waters,*
> *You restoreth my soul.*
> *You guideth me in the paths of righteousness for your*
> *   name's sake.*

Yea, though I walk through the valley of the shadow of death
   I shall fear no evil,
For you are with me;
Your rod and your staff, they comfort me.
You preparest a table before me in the presence of mine enemies;
You hast anointed my head with oil; my cup runneth over.
Surely goodness and mercy shall follow me all the days of my life;
And I shall dwell in your house forever.

A Prayer of Affirmation

The mid-1980s, when I lived in rural Alabama, was one of the few times in my life when I had good health insurance. Therefore, I was ever faithful about a yearly physical and mammogram. When a mammogram showed some irregularities, my young doctor informed me that I needed an operation to remove an egg-yolk-shaped section from my left breast. I was a wreck and began calling all my nuns/sisters who had anything to do with a hospital to gather some information. They calmed me down, and I decided to go to Birmingham for a second opinion. During the week of my trauma, I happened to turn on our little black-and-white television set and saw an interview with Louise Hay and Dr. Bernie Siegel that featured their respective books, *You Can Heal Your Life* and *Love, Medicine and Miracles.* As it turned out, the hospital in Birmingham discovered that the irregularities in my breast were the size of grains of salt—not an egg yolk—and they were nonmalignant. From that time on, I began to accept the responsibility for my own health. In times of stress or ill health, I look to Louise Hay's counsel and say the affirmations she suggests on my prayer beads. You might say I'm praying myself into a new way of living.

Deep at the center of my being there is an infinite well of Love.
I now allow this Love to flow to the surface.
It fills my heart, my body, my mind, my consciousness, my
very being,
and radiates out from me in all directions and returns to me
multiplied.
The more Love I use and give, the more I have to give,
the supply is endless.[1]

A Prayer of Forgiveness

All of my life, I have struggled with letting go of resentment. But I was given a mother who does not know the meaning of the word *resentment*. I remember as a kid going to bed *furious* with her, swearing that I would never speak with her again. The next morning, however, I would go down to breakfast, and there she would be—greeting me cheerfully, as if we had never had a fight. I would forget my pledge of the night before, figuring that I could always go through with it the next time. (And there always was a next time!) But I never could keep that pledge because it just wasn't in my mother's nature to hold a grudge. So when I came across this prayer that was found scribbled on a piece of wrapping paper near the body of a dead child at the Ravensbruck concentration camp in Germany, I marveled at the depth of insight and compassion that has always escaped me. Praying these words opens my heart and stretches my mind to the power of forgiveness.

[O God], remember not only
the men and women of goodwill,
but also those of ill will.
But do not remember all the suffering

they have inflicted on us;
remember the fruits we have bought,
thanks to this suffering—
our comradeship, our loyalty,
our humility, our courage,
our generosity, the greatness of heart which has grown out of
    all this,
and when they come to judgment
let all the fruits which we have borne
be their forgiveness. Amen.[2]

A Prayer for Purpose

I am attracted to this prayer by Alice Bailey because it assumes that there is a plan for all of life that I do not understand. It celebrates that all of life has a meaning and honors those among us who are masters of love. When I pray these words, I join my little self to a purpose greater than what I see around me.

The Great Invocation

From the point of Light within the Mind of God
Let light stream forth into human minds.
Let Light descend on Earth.

From the point of Love within the Heart of God
Let love stream forth into human hearts.
May the Coming One return to Earth.

From the centre where the Will of God is known
Let purpose guide all little human wills—
The purpose which the Masters know and serve.

From the center which we call the human race
Let the Plan of Love and Light work out
And may it seal the door where evil dwells.

Let Light and Love and Power restore the Plan on Earth.

A Prayer of Hope

I remember my aunt Catherine sitting in her rocking chair with the radio on, listening to the Boston Red Sox, and praying the rosary for them to win. I wonder whether she ever got discouraged. You see, she died in 1982, which was a good twenty-two years before her big prayer was answered. She had a slew of holy cards and a collection of prayers that she kept in a small book encircled by a rubber band. This prayer for contentment, credited to St. Therese of Lisieux, the Little Flower, is one I keep in my own "small book."

Today, may there be peace within.
May we trust our highest power that we are exactly where we
    are meant to be.
May we not forget the infinite possibilities that are born
    of faith.
May we use those gifts that we have received, and pass on the
    love that has been given to us.
May we be content knowing we are of God.
May this Presence settle in our bones,
and allow our souls the freedom to sing, dance, and to bask in
    the sun.
The Presence is there for each and every one of us.

A Prayer for Clarity

When I was training to be a sister, one of my favorite people was a nun named Pachomia. She was a brilliant mathematician, still teaching math in her late eighties. I once asked her why she had never gone on for her doctorate. She looked at me and said, "Why would I spend seven years learning more than anyone ever needs to know about a tiny subject, when I could get yet another master's degree and broaden my base of knowledge?" I still smile when I repeat one of the favorite prayers of this wise mentor.

> *Grant me the senility to forget the people I never liked anyway,*
> *The good fortune to run into the ones I do,*
> *And the eyesight to tell the difference.*

A Prayer of Comfort

When I first learned about the Jewish custom of reciting the Kaddish following the death of a loved one, I was amazed: There is absolutely no reference to death in the entire prayer! Rather, the theme is an ode to the greatness of God, honoring the One who created such a soul and to whom that soul has returned. Perhaps that is the greatest comfort we could ever have at such a loss.

> *Only through You can we transcend the limits of time forever.*
> *Exalted and hallowed be God's greatness*
> *In this world of Your creation.*
> *May Your will be fulfilled*
> *And Your sovereignty revealed*
> *In the days of our lifetime*
> *And the life of the whole house of Israel*
> *And say, Amen*

May You be blessed forever.
Even to all eternity.
May You, most Holy One, be blessed,
Praised and honored, extolled and glorified,
Adored and exalted above all else.
Blessed are You
Beyond all blessings and hymns, praises and consolations
That may be uttered in this world,
And say, Amen.
May peace abundant descend from heaven
With life for us and for all Israel,
And say, Amen.
May God, who makes peace on high,
Bring peace to us and to all Israel,
And say,
Amen.[3]

A Prayer of Trust

In her book *The Places That Scare You: A Guide to Fearlessness in Difficult Times*, Buddhist nun Pema Chödrön talks about her teacher's encouragement to go to "the places that scare you." I often recite Pema's suggested chant, a traditional Tibetan Buddhist blessing, when I feel afraid.

The Four Limitless Ones

May all sentient beings enjoy happiness and the root of happiness.
May we be free from suffering and the root of suffering.
May we not be separated from the great happiness devoid of
suffering.

May we dwell in the great equanimity free from passion,
aggression, and prejudice.[4]

A Prayer of Blessing

Macrina Wiederkehr's prayer "Final Blessing," from her book *The Song of the Seed*, reminds me of the Chinese concept of yin and yang, the two primal opposing, but complementary, forces found in everything in the universe, each needing the other to exist. There is no birth without death. There is no full without empty. There are no butterflies without caterpillars. What brings us the most pleasure has the potential of bringing the most pain. What brings us the most pain likewise holds the potential of giving us the most joy. When I pray this prayer, I am in touch with the breadth of the Holy.

Final Blessing
May there always be a little light in your darkness,
May there always be a little faith in your doubt.
May there always be a little joy in your sorrow,
May there always be a little light in your dying.
May there always be a little hope in your despair,
May there always be a little courage in your fear.
May there always be a little slow in your hurry.[5]

A Daily Prayer

The first prayer that I ever learned from my aunt Catherine was the Lord's Prayer, or the Our Father. About ten years ago, I came across a translation by Neil Douglas-Klotz, a member of the Sufi Order of the West, of this prayer that touched me so deeply that I began to use it in my daily prayer.

The Lord's Prayer

O thou, the Breath, the Light of all,

Let this Light create a heart-shrine within.

And your Counsel rule 'til Oneness guides me.

Your One Desire then acts with mine, as in all light, so in all forms.

Grant what I need each day, in bread and insight.

Loose the cords of mistakes binding me, as I

release the strands I hold of other's faults.

Do not let surface things delude me.

But keep me from unripe acts.

To you belongs the ruling mind,

the life that can act and do,

the song that beautifies all,

from age to age it renews.

In faith, I will to be true.[6]

Another Daily Prayer

Another prayer I use daily is one that Mychal Judge loved. Mychal was a Catholic chaplain to the New York City fire department; he died while giving a final blessing to firefighters in the World Trade Center on September 11, 2001. I find that, in the end, this is really the core of all that matters.

> *[God,] take me where You want me to go;*
>
> *Let me meet whom You want me to meet;*
>
> *Tell me what You want me to say;*
>
> *and keep me out of Your way.*[7]

Secret 5

Interconnectedness Gives Prayer Life

Prayer may not change things for you,
but it for sure changes you for things.
—Samuel M. Shoemaker

As campus minister at an all-girls high school outside Chicago, I once took a group of young women on a service spring break to Appalachia. We joined young men from a nearby Chicago high school and, accompanied by several parents, who included several skilled craftsmen and a cook, we took on the task of building a house in a "holler" in Kentucky.

One day after working on the house, one of the local men offered to take us to the top of a nearby mountain. There were no roads, but he had a big four-wheeler and assured us that it was perfect for climbing. When we got to the top, the campus minister from the boys' school (whom the girls referred to as a "hunk") informed us that he was a Scout leader and offered to take the students on a small hike. The local man and I decided to stay and forage for morels.

About an hour later, after collecting a good amount of morels, we returned to the truck expecting to see the students. None were in sight. Another hour passed, and still no students. The month was April, so the sun was slowly inching down the mountain, taking what light there was with it. When I expressed my growing concern to my Kentucky friend, he reassured me that any Scout leader would know how to get down the mountain by following the creek—eventually it would flow into a larger body of water, and thus civilization.

I was unconvinced, but without any other option, we took the truck and headed back down the mountain. Just as we were about to reach a road, we saw a ragged bunch of teens, scratched and exhausted, and a very relieved-looking "hunk." They clambered into the back of the truck and nursed their scratches and bruises, which were legion, for they were all in short pants. The highlight of their day was a scrambled-egg-and-morel supper and an adventure to share with their parents when they got home. The highlight for me was that I did not have to "share" a story with parents about their missing children. The lesson for all of us was to remember to follow water downhill if we ever got lost.

Water, the essence of life, the substance that makes up 70 percent of earth and of our bodies, flows downhill. But what if there is no "downhill"? What happens to water when there is no place to go? The lowest place on earth is the body of water we call the Dead Sea. The River Jordan and several other smaller streams flow into this sea, but because it is fourteen hundred feet below sea level, the water has no way to exit. The only way water leaves the sea is by evaporation: It disappears into thin air and makes clouds, leaving behind a body of water with such high salt levels that it cannot support life.

Prayer, like water, is meant to flow, but it needs to flow *somewhere* or it loses its "prayerness," its life-giving essence. It stays just words. Of necessity, prayer must lead to some sort of creative healing of the world, or it becomes like the Dead Sea: It doesn't sustain life. Prayer must be accompanied by some sort of action. Prayer without growth, prayer without challenging situations of oppression, prayer for the status quo in unloving situations is dead prayer. Prayer must lead to a place where we can "repair the world," the task called *tikkun olam* in Hebrew. If there is no *tikkun olam* in our life, our prayer, like water with no outlet, becomes dead.

We do need time alone in silence, in contemplation. But if we have *only* time alone, if we do not understand that our relationship with the Divine leads us to heal the world, then our prayer lacks an outlet and our spirit deadens.

The Principle of Communion

> The life I touch for good or ill will touch another life, and
> that in turn another, until who knows where the trembling
> stops or in what far place my touch will be felt.
>
> —*Frederick Buechner*

If I were to stop with the statement that we need to "heal the world," you and I would both be overwhelmed. The task is obviously far beyond what we could do individually! But, in truth, we are called to a much greater consciousness; one that, paradoxically, is within our reach. One of the secrets of prayer lies in the interconnectedness of all of creation: Our individual prayers add to the energy of other people's prayers, and together, they have far-reaching effects beyond what we can control or predict.

Recently a friend sent me a beautiful invocation written by Dr. Ingrid L. Schafer that she gave at the Oklahoma Academy of Science.[1] Whenever I read it, I fantasize about teaching a science class that begins with this prayer of thanksgiving, and having the class spend the year working our way through it.

In Memory

Lawrence K. ("Larry") Magrath, PhD
Professor of Biology and Interdisciplinary Studies
University of Science & Arts of Oklahoma

Let us give thanks for chaos and logos and implicate order;
for dark matter, bright galaxies, and nonlocal connections;
for crystals and continents;
for Lucy's skull and Mary Leakey's footprints in volcanic ash;
for Thales' water, Heraclitus' fire, and Pythagorean forms;
for the Indian zero, algebra, and algorithms;
for the oscillations of the Yin *and* Yang;
for acupuncture, Su Sung's astronomical clock, and Huang Tau
  P'o's textile technology;
for Arabic alchemists on the Old Silk Road and Ibn Sina's
  Canon of Medicine;
for Euclid and Newton and "God playing dice";
for Kepler's snowflake and Kekulè's dream;
for Mendel's monastery peas and the genetic Tetragrammaton
  on the spiral staircase of life;
for fractals, ferns, and fall foliage;
for caterpillars and cocoons;
for the infant's first cry;

for Pachelbel's canon;

*for stained glass windows, Leeuwenhoek's microscope, and the
    Galileo probe;*

*for the World Wide Web to help us become conscious of cosmic
    interconnectedness;*

*but most of all, let us give thanks for the twin passions which
    make us fully human—*

*the yearning to transcend the boundaries of time and space by
    learning and by loving.*

Even if we don't understand all the references in this prayer, we
can certainly grasp the interconnectedness it suggests—that we are
joined with each other and with every other form of life in an amazing cosmic dance. But there is more to our connectedness than just
an abstract concept. Interdependence is vital for survival. The communion between plants and the soil, water and sunlight, sustains life
on this planet. The total food chain is dependent on each part being
there. If the tiniest part of the chain is destroyed, the largest part will
be affected.

For example, humpback whales eat krill (tiny crustaceans),
plankton (microscopic plants and animals), and small fish. Slight
temperature changes affect the microscopic algae first. Their disappearance leads to a domino effect that causes a similar change
nearby, which causes another similar change, and so on, analogous
to a falling row of dominoes. When the tiny fish lose their food
source, they in turn disappear. Likewise, the whales dependent on
these tiny fish begin to struggle. Ultimately, the domino effect will
lead to the disappearance of whales in that area of the ocean, and
then what affects nonhumans begins to affect humans.

This concept of interdependence is part of what Thomas Berry considers one of the three basic principles of the universe, and he calls it "communion." Communion essentially means that everyone and everything has the ability to relate to every other person or thing, that everything in the universe is bound together on a cosmic level in an inseparable relationship. Take the electromagnetic force: It is communion on a cosmic level because it binds the electrons to the nucleus to form atoms. Or consider that all beings on the planet breathe the same air and drink the same water.

To become present to Earth, to the cosmos, is to enter into an intimate relationship with all of creation, to experience this physical communion. All spiritual practices are linked in the same way, though they use different images, metaphors, or stories. And this is key to our understanding of prayer because it means that *every* prayer is linked; every prayer has an effect on the cosmos, every prayer matters.

One of the smallest and most powerful books I own is *The Hundredth Monkey*, written by Ken Keyes Jr. In it, Keyes describes what has become known as the "hundredth monkey effect." During the last century, a group of scientists studied the Japanese monkey species *Macaca fuscata* on the island of Koshima. In one experiment, sweet potatoes were dropped onto the island. The monkeys liked the taste of the sweet potatoes but not the sand that covered them. One day, a young female monkey began to wash her potato in a nearby stream, and she then taught her mother and her playmates, who in turn taught their mothers. Gradually, many of the monkeys learned to wash the sand off the sweet potatoes—but not all. Several years later, something startling took place. The researchers observed that once a critical number of monkeys were washing their sweet potatoes—the so-called hundredth monkey—the behavior instantly spread to all the monkeys on the island. The scientists surmised that the energy from that one additional monkey somehow caused an ideological breakthrough. When a certain critical number achieved an awareness, this new awareness was communicated from mind to mind. Then something even more surprising happened: Monkeys on the other islands and the mainland *all* began washing their sweet potatoes. The energy had leapt over the sea!

Although the critical number may vary, the "hundredth monkey effect" suggests that when a restricted number of people know of a new way to approach a problem, that way will remain in the consciousness of just those people. But there is a tipping point when the addition of one more person receiving the new information makes the energy field so strong that the information is available to be picked up by almost everyone!

When it comes to prayer, any one of us, at any time, may be the hundredth monkey. Any one of our prayers might be the added energy needed to create change. Every prayer matters. Every action matters.

But I hasten to add that I'm talking about "action" from an expansive viewpoint. If you're thinking that action means being an activist, yes, for some it does. But we don't all need to join a political protest or enlist in the Peace Corps to have an effect; some of us are called to just "stand there" in prayer.

A "Connecting" Prayer Exercise

Read these words of cosmologist Brian Swimme, from *The Universe Is a Green Dragon* and hold them in your mind and heart for a few minutes:

> The basic dynamism of the universe is the attraction each
> galaxy has for every other galaxy. Nothing in all science has

been established and studied with greater attention and detail than this primary attraction of each part of the universe for every other part.[2]

Then consider all of life that surrounds you—animal, human, plant, even Earth itself. Let your mind imagine being "attracted" to each form of life that crosses your thoughts. Let your connectedness to all things sink in and offer a prayer of thanks to your Creator.

Stand There

Certain thoughts are prayers. There are
moments when, whatever be the attitude
of the body, the soul is on its knees.
—*Victor Hugo,* Les Misérables

A few months after I entered the novitiate, I read about an event that occurred on Block Island, just off the coast of Rhode Island. On August 12, 1970, Block Island became the focal point of every newspaper in the country. One of the FBI's most wanted criminals, Jesuit priest Daniel Berrigan, was arrested there. Berrigan had been sentenced to prison for three years for burning draft files, but he had refused to serve his time and had gone underground. Much to the FBI's great embarrassment, they could not seem to apprehend Berrigan, although he frequently showed up briefly at public events, made impromptu speeches, and then went back into hiding.

When the FBI finally caught up with Berrigan and escorted him to a ferry that would take him to prison, someone took a picture of the three men: two seriously unhappy agents and a peaceful, smiling prisoner. I had a six-foot poster of that picture on the back of my door in my bedroom at the novitiate, and the caption read, "Don't just do something, stand there!"

It is a paradoxical statement: It seems opposed to common sense, and yet it carries truth. Figuratively speaking, a paradox is similar to an oxymoron. *Oxy* is the Greek word for "sharp" and *moros* is the word for "dull," so an oxymoron is something that has two contradictory attributes, such as a healthy tan, a plastic glass, a calm storm, a safety hazard, or a just war.

The well-known Japanese Buddhist koan, "What is the sound of one hand clapping?" presents a paradoxical question. The paradox is the "logic" underlying the phenomena that when people know they have a limited time to live, they begin to truly *live*. As Etty Hillesum, the Dutch mystic whose life ended at age twenty-nine when she was at Auschwitz, wrote, "By excluding death from our life we cannot live a full life, and by admitting death into our life we enlarge and enrich it."[3]

Paradox is perhaps the safest way to speak about the unspeakable. Before I began to comprehend the paradox of "don't just do something, stand there," I thought that nuns who stayed in their convents and prayed all day were wasting their lives. They did not appear to "do" anything. When I began to grasp the dynamic energy involved in meditation and prayer, I slowly started to understand how important it is for them to *be* there, to "stand there" in prayer for the world. Today I know I do not wish to live in a world without prayer meditators. I rely heavily on their standing there as witness to another reality.

There are times when we know, viscerally, the power of just standing there. For instance, when we are with someone who is grieving, no words can really comfort. Our being there, our presence—with all of our inadequacies—is gift enough. When my friend Lynn's son,

David, was killed on September 11, 2001, a friend she had not seen in a long time approached her with arms wide open and hugged her wordlessly. The friend stood with Lynn as a healing presence, and that wordless hug conveyed all that could be said or done at that point.

Then there's Rosa Parks: She did not do anything; she just sat there. She did not move when she was asked to give her seat to a white man. Rosa Parks took what Gandhi called "an action in the passive." She did not do anything to support a system that she knew was unjust. Paradoxically, her nonaction moved a country to action. The civil rights movement began in a very public way, and the United States became more of a "land of the free and home of the brave."

At its core, I believe the concept of "stand there" means to live as we pray and pray as we live. I think of the story of the priest who couldn't speak Spanish well:

> A priest was assigned to a parish in South America. He had studied at the language school and must have done just enough to pass, but he slaughtered the language every time he spoke from the pulpit. When a bishop visited this little parish, he strongly encouraged the priest to continue studying the language so the people could understand him better. The priest promised to work on it.
>
> A couple of years later the bishop returned and slid into the back pew of the church to hear how the priest had improved. There appeared to be no discernable change in the priest's mastery of the language.
>
> The bishop turned to the man sitting beside him and asked, "Do you understand what the priest is preaching about?"

The man looked up at the bishop and said confidently, "Of course!"

The bishop was confounded. He confessed to the man that he himself could understand little of the sermon.

"Oh," replied the man, "I can't understand a word he is saying. But I see what he does. He helps us build, he visits the sick, he's with us in our sorrow, and parties with us in our joy. I don't know what he says, but I know what he means."

This marvelous story echoes the teaching of St. Francis, who told his brothers, "Preach the Gospel at all times and use words if you have to." In other words, our lives should be our real preaching, our real prayers. I think of Søren Kierkegaard's astute statement that "the function of prayer is ... to change the nature of the one who prays."

A fulfilling prayer practice can strengthen our inner spirit, help us to hold true to our convictions, and give us the courage to follow through with what we know in our hearts to be right, even if nothing seems to be different, externally, because of our prayers, as this brief story captures:

Shout to Keep Safe—And Certain

A prophet once came to a city to convert its inhabitants. At first the people listened to his sermons, but they gradually drifted away till there was not a single soul to hear the prophet when he spoke.

One day a traveler said to him, "Why do you go on preaching?"

Said the prophet, "In the beginning I hoped to change these people. If I still shout it is only to prevent them from changing me."[4]

The effectiveness of our prayers cannot always be measured by tangible results outside ourselves. Sometimes we need to continue to "shout" even when our shouting appears fruitless. Who knows when our prayer will become the "hundredth" prayer that changes the people and communities we love? Who knows when our "stand there" will shift us, or someone else, to "do something"?

A "Stand There" Prayer Exercise

Think of someone you do not like, or someone with whom you need a healing. Picture that person the happiest, most contented you have ever seen her or him to be. Hold out your arms to her or him in a wordless embrace. Pray for that person's healing and well-being. Let your prayer flow out of you and encircle her or him with light. Hold this picture for as long as you can. Ask for the peace of God to fill both of you.

Do Something

We must no longer see prayer as preparation for action. Prayer must be understood as action itself, a way of responding.... Prayer is not undertaken instead of other actions, but as a foundation for all the rest of the actions we take.

—Jim Wallis

Several years ago, I received an unusual Christmas card from Mary, one of my mentors. Every year her card contains a prayer/poem/consciousness-raiser, and that year it was a prayer by Ann Weems, a poet from St. Louis, Missouri. It was a beautiful reminder that we were celebrating the one who taught us that loving the invisible means taking care of the visible.

People such as us, who live in plenty—who have to go out of our way to see anyone who is without the physical necessities of life; who decide *what* we shall eat, not *whether* we can eat; who complain about the price of gas as we drive alone in vehicles that were meant to carry four or five others; who throw away two to three large bags of trash *every* week; who buy water in plastic bottles when our tap water is perfectly safe—need reminders such as this prayer by Weems.

We Pray This Day

O God, we pray this day:
for all who have a song they cannot sing,
for all who have a burden they cannot bear,
for all who live in chains they cannot break,
for all who wander homeless and cannot return,
for those who are sick and for those who tend them,
for those who wait for loved ones
  and wait in vain,
for those who live in hunger
  and for those who will not share their bread,
for those who are misunderstood
  and for those who misunderstand,
for those who are captives and for those who are captors,
for those whose words of love are locked within their hearts
  and for those who yearn to hear those words.

Have mercy upon these, O God,
Have mercy upon us all.[5]

This prayer leads right into another. St. Francis of Assisi looked at a church that was consumed with wealth and power, and he offered another way to be in this world. St. Francis challenged the status quo and prayed that the comfortable would be made uncomfortable.

May you be blessed with discomfort at easy answers,
half truths and superficial relationships,
so that you may live deep within your heart.
May you be blessed with anger at injustice,
oppression and exploitation of people,
so that you may work for justice, freedom and peace.
May you be blessed with tears to shed
for those who suffer from pain, rejection, starvation and war,
so that you may reach out your hand
to comfort them and to turn their pain into joy
And may you be blessed with enough foolishness
to believe that you can make a difference in this world,
so that you can do what others claim cannot be done!

This kind of prayer catalyzes "stand there" into action. There are times when our prayer will necessarily lead us to "reach out" our hand to "make a difference in this world." When Daniel Berrigan stood against the powers of the U.S. government over and over again, to bear witness that the war in Vietnam was against his principles, his prayer life and his action became one.

Each of us needs to follow where our prayers lead us, and sometimes it leads us to say no! as Berrigan did. I think of what German theologian Dorothee Soelle wrote in *The Silent Cry.*

In my search for concepts that depict the possibilities open to mystics of their relation to the world, I find a series of different options. They lie between withdrawal from the world and the transformation of the world through revolution. But whether it be withdrawal, renunciation, disagreement, divergence, dissent, reform, resistance, rebellion or revolution, in all of these forms there is a No! to the world as it exists now.[6]

Sometimes we need to say no by confronting interlocking systems of oppression. By this I mean the structures that exist in our culture to give unearned assets to some and to disadvantage others in the areas of race, ethnicity, gender, sexual orientation, class, economic access, age, and religion.

We can confront oppression even in the very *language* of our prayer. When we use the term *we*, for example, we need to intentionally identify who the "we" includes. Women should no longer have to play a guessing game, wondering whether "we" are included or not. When the Declaration of Independence was written, the phrase "all men are created equal" literally meant only white, property-owning men. But surely the "us" in Jesus's teaching prayer, "Give us this day our daily bread," includes all women and men. Our prayers need to use inclusive words, to clearly embrace everyone.

Sometimes we need to say no by testing the rules, the accepted norms. Here's another of de Mello's wonderful tales that demonstrates how someone with a prayer practice can gain the confidence needed to break the rules and regulations that hinder wholistic living, to do what is right even in the face of adversity.

The Monk and the Woman

Two Buddhist monks, on their way to a monastery, found an exceedingly beautiful woman at the riverbank. Like them, she wished to cross the river, but the water was too high. So one of the monks lifted her onto his back and carried her across.

His fellow monk was thoroughly scandalized. For two hours he berated him on his negligence in keeping the rule: Had he forgotten he was a monk? How did he dare touch a woman? And worse, carry her across the river? What would people say? Had he not brought their holy religion into disrepute? And so on.

The offending monk patiently listened to the neverending sermon. Finally he broke in with "Brother, I dropped that woman at the river. Are you still carrying her?"[7]

Although de Mello does not describe these two monks, their conversation suggests their level of experience and therefore their ages. The monk who thinks that the rule is to be obeyed to the letter is young; he does not understand the spirit of the rule. I think of the other monk as older, more experienced, someone who has what I call the grace of aging; he no doubt is a product of serious prayer. What preoccupied him in his twenties is no longer of concern to him. He used to see the world as either this or that, but now he understands the gray areas of life, the ambiguity that makes up the real stuff of our lives. A consistent prayer practice can bring this type of freedom because a steady connection with the Divine will hold us in good stead when we face life choices.

Whatever shape our *no* takes, we need to act with compassion. Sometimes, as I have been writing this book on prayer, I ask myself,

"If I become impatient with my mother, who lives with me, because I'm 'too busy,' and if by my impatience, I add to the burden she already bears in her aging body, what am I really doing? Where is my compassion?"

The level of our compassion affects our prayer life, and our prayer life affects our compassion. In the Christian scripture there is a saying of Jesus that is often translated as "Be perfect as your Heavenly Father is perfect." I have always found this to be an impossible goal. A friend of mine who studies biblical languages informed me that a closer translation of that command would read, "Be *compassionate* as your Heavenly Father is compassionate."

One of my favorite stories about the effect of compassion is one I originally read in M. Scott Peck's *The Road Less Traveled*. It is an old story and often retold, and I have adapted the tale to reflect a reality closer to home for me.

The Rabbi's Gift

There was a convent that had fallen upon hard times. Once a great religious order, antimonastic persecution in the seventeenth and eighteenth centuries had decimated the community, and there were only five nuns left in the decaying motherhouse: the abbess and four other women, all over the age of seventy. Clearly the order was dying.

In the deep woods surrounding the convent, there was a little hut that a rabbi from a nearby town occasionally used for a hermitage. Although they had never met him, the old nuns could always sense when the rabbi was in his hermitage. "The rabbi is in the woods; the rabbi is in the woods again," they would whisper to each other.

As the abbess agonized over the coming demise of her community, it occurred to her to visit the hermitage and ask the rabbi if, by some possible chance, he could offer any advice that might save the order.

The rabbi welcomed the abbess at his hut. But when the abbess explained the purpose of her visit, the rabbi could only commiserate with her. "I know how it is," he exclaimed. "The spirit has gone out of the people. It is the same in my town. Almost no one comes to the synagogue anymore."

So the old abbess and the old rabbi wept together. Then they read parts of the Torah and quietly spoke of deep things. The time came when the abbess had to leave, and they embraced each other.

"It has been a wonderful thing that we should meet after all these years," the abbess said, "but I have still failed in my purpose for coming here. Is there nothing you can tell me, no piece of advice you can give me, that would help me save my order?"

"No, I am sorry," the rabbi responded. "I have no advice to give. The only thing I can tell you is that the Messiah is one of you."

When the abbess returned to the convent, the nuns gathered around her, asking, "Well, what did the rabbi say?"

"He couldn't help," the abbess replied. "We just wept and read the Torah together. The only thing he did say, just as I was leaving … it was something cryptic. He said that the Messiah is one of us. I don't know what he meant."

The old nuns pondered this and each wondered whether there was any possible significance to the rabbi's words. The Messiah is one of *us*? Could the rabbi possibly have meant one of the nuns in the convent? If that were the case, which one? In the days and weeks that followed, the nuns began to treat each other with extraordinary respect on the off chance that one among them might be the Messiah.

Because the forest in which the convent was situated was beautiful, people still occasionally came to visit the grounds to picnic on the lawn, to wander the paths, and even, now and then, to go to pray in the dilapidated chapel. As they did so, without even being conscious of it, they sensed the aura of extraordinary respect that now began to surround the five old nuns. It seemed to radiate out from them and permeate the atmosphere of the place, and there was something strangely attractive, even compelling, about it. Hardly knowing why, they began to come back to the convent more frequently to picnic, to play, and to pray. Then they began bringing their friends to show them this special place. And their friends brought their friends.

Gradually, some of the younger women who came to visit the convent started to talk more and more with the old nuns. After a while, one asked if she could join them. Then another. Then another. Within a few years the convent once again became a thriving order and, thanks to the rabbi's gift, a vibrant center of light and spirituality.

The Messiah is one of us! What if each of us thought of ourselves as a "messiah"? Would we not treat ourselves and our neighbors with more patience and love? Would we not pray with more compassion, more kindness, more respect?

There is a Buddhist *metta* (from the Pali word meaning "loving-kindness for oneself and for others") that I often use to keep me conscious of the call to compassion. I say it first for myself using the pronoun *I;* then I repeat it using *you* for every member of my family and also for people with whom I struggle. (When I use it with a large group, I change the pronoun to *we.*)

Lovingkindness Meditation

May I be at peace.
May my heart remain open.
May I awaken to the light of my own true nature.
May I be healed.
May I be a source of healing for others.

Ultimately, whether our prayers lead us to "stand there" or to "do something," we are each a source of healing for others. We are each the source of *tikkun olam,* of healing the world, which may well be the most important task of our time.

A "Do Something" Prayer Exercise

Consider a person with whom you have a difficult time. Picture once again your prayer flowing out of you, reaching this person and embracing her or him in a bath of compassion. Then ponder this statement: *The level of your compassion affects your prayer life, and your prayer life affects your compassion.* Let the flow of your compassion spread farther and see where it leads you. Consider how you might make a tangible difference for this person today.

Secret 6

To Learn about Prayer, You Need to Pray

> We can read all the books that have ever been written about prayer, but until we actually choose ... to pray, we will never learn.
>
> —*Hope MacDonald*

There is an old story told about not being able to help anyone find God because it would be like helping a fish find water. Sometimes I think the story could be applied to helping people pray. We are immersed in the presence, and yet we keep on looking. We are filled with the divine spark, and yet we seek elsewhere. Perhaps it is time to plumb our own depths.

In a paper published by the Wellesley Centers for Women, Peggy MacIntosh writes about "Feeling Like a Fraud." Many of us feel that way when it comes to prayer. We may think we don't know the "right" words to say. Or we may believe that only a few, such as saints or gurus or prophets, can compose prayers. Perhaps we have been raised in a

117

tradition that taught rote prayers, not personal, direct prayers. Some might believe that God lives in certain places and that prayers will only count if we are in those sacred places where the presence is felt.

How do we move from other people's words to being able to trust ourselves to use our own words? And what should we say? It depends, very much, on our belief system.

Approaching the Divine

Start seeing everything as God, But keep it a secret.

—Hafiz

From the time my aunt Catherine began to teach me prayers by rote, I began to understand the concept that there was a personal God with whom I could communicate. People who follow the Abrahamic traditions of Judaism, Christianity, and Islam are usually comfortable with the idea that we can have a relationship with a personal being, and they tend to anthropomorphize the Divine. Many Christians, for example, use the anthropomorphic terms father and son. Many Western churches depict the Divine in a familiar visual form—think Michelangelo and the Sistine Chapel or L. C. Tiffany and his stained-glass windows. These are images of God with attributes familiar to human beings, a God with emotions of love, anger, sorrow, and judgment.

Others are more comfortable with a transpersonal concept of God as a force underlying all things, a God "without attributes," as Sri Ramakrishna, the nineteenth-century Hindu avatar, expressed it. I have to admit that it took me a very long time to accept that my personal concept of God was way too small for the God of the cosmos. In some ways I had been so indoctrinated with the concept of a personal God that to incorporate the idea of a transpersonal God felt as if I were losing a relationship, rather than expanding my understanding of the Divine.

I remember being shocked when I heard that Cornell University scientist Carl Sagan did not believe in God. What I later came to realize, as I struggled with the concept of a nonpersonal presence, was that Sagan could not believe in the personal God that is presented in the Abrahamic traditions of Judaism, Christianity, and Islam. Yet Sagan charged our Western culture with awe of the cosmos with his public television series of the same name. How could he possibly have reduced that belief to fit a limited "old, bearded (and, in Western countries, white) man in the sky" view?

Whatever our concept of God, it will be reflected in the way we address God, in what is referred to as "Godtalk." Even a cursory look at the prayer practices of different faith traditions reveals many ways to speak about the Holy. For example, the Orthodox Jewish community uses a hyphen (-) between the letters G and D to represent the Jewish belief that one can never really know G-d in G-d's entirety. Some traditional Jews also never speak the word *God*, believing the sacred is too holy for us to pronounce.

In the Orthodox tradition, one must never make representations of God in any way—even in speech. Yet I suggest that by using only the masculine pronoun when referring to God or other metaphors like the term *Lord*, a representation is indeed made. The representation that God is male. Personally, I prefer the name for God used by Elisabeth Schüssler Fiorenza, the Krister Stendahl Professor of Divinity at Harvard University Divinity School. Schüssler Fiorenza prefers the spelling *G*d* because it suggests that, as humans, our ideas of and names for God are ambiguous and inadequate. It also allows for a God without male or female characteristics.

In Hebrew scripture (also known as the Torah to Jews, or the Old Testament to Christians), the initials YHWH are used to denote God. As the story goes, when God appeared to Moses at the burning bush, the holy name was revealed to Moses as YHWH, a collection of consonants that, when pronounced, sounds like the rushing of air through the mouth. It is usually translated as "Is-Was-Will-Be" or "I will be what I shall be." The fact that the common translation of YHWH is a verb, indicating action, fascinates me. Nothing static here!

Thomas Cahill notes in his book *The Gifts of the Jews* that in the Middle Ages, the name of God became so sacred that it was never uttered. Since that time, traditional Jews use the terms *Adonai,* meaning "the Lord," or *ha-Shem,* meaning "the Name" when referring to God.

In the Middle East, anyone who speaks Arabic, whether Christian, Jewish, or Muslim, uses the term *Allah* when speaking of God. Many think that Allah is exclusively an Islamic term, but Allah is the Arabic word for God worshiped by anyone from monotheistic traditions.

One thing I keep coming back to is something that Joyce Rupp wrote in her book *Prayers to Sophia*:

> All our names for the Divine ... are inadequate. All these metaphors
> are our feeble human attempts and projections as we try to draw
> near to the Mysterious One.... In order to have a personal rela-
> tionship, however, it is helpful to name the Divine.[1]

The whole idea of a personal relationship with God, of direct contact with the Holy, can, however, pose a problem for some, depending on their religious traditions. Some of us come from traditions that call for an intermediary between God and ourselves. Some grapple with self-doubt, trusting others more than ourselves. Even the term *spiritual*

director is an oxymoron because it suggests that someone outside ourselves can "direct" us in our spiritual life. (I hasten to add that good
spiritual directors understand that this is not true, that they are companions on the road.)

Some give their power away to gurus, which makes them very
vulnerable to betrayal. Kabir, one of India's best-known mystic poets
of the fifteenth century, proposed that the titles guru, swami, master,
teacher, yogi, and priest often suggest peacocks. Kabir recommended
we give them a litmus test: Hold them upside down over a cliff, and if
they don't wet their pants, perhaps they deserve the title. I love this hu-
morous encouragement to rely on our own ways to communicate with
God directly and not to give our power over to another.

I have watched people's faith crumble as their intermediaries to
the Divine, the priests whom they thought were truly God's represen-
tatives on earth, have been accused of horrendous crimes and sins
against children. It is an unfortunate occurrence in any situation where
people give their entire trust to another human being. The emphasis is
on the word *human*. There is no right person who has all the answers
to guide us. There is no right book on prayer that will give us all the
answers for which we long. There are no right words to say when addressing the Divine.

Dr. Margery Resnick, associate professor of foreign languages and
literature at MIT, has suggested that Teresa of Ávila, one of the most significant mystics and teachers on the spiritual life, followed a long-stand-
ing tradition of relating to the Divine without any "middleman." She had
come from a family of Jewish *conversos* (people who were forced to convert to Christianity during the Inquisition), and Jews had always dealt directly with God. Because Teresa trusted her experience with the Divine,
she believed in direct communication with God in prayer and meditation.

Though the temptation to look outside ourselves is overwhelming, it is time for us to look within, to trust that spark of the Holy of which the Kabbalah speaks.

A New Approach Exercise

One way to enrich your prayer life is to try out some of the names other people and religions have given the Divine. Try names that are outside your traditional vocabulary. You might consider the ninety-nine names, or attributes, Muslims use for the Holy One. I keep a list of these names in my office because I find them so very meaningful—especially in this time of great misunderstanding about what Muslims believe. I've listed the names here in English (in Arabic, the written words themselves are works of art!), and I encourage you to prayerfully consider them, being especially aware of what images of God come alive for you as you say each name and of new ways you feel connected to the Holy.

The All-Compassionate, the All-Merciful, the Absolute Ruler, the Pure One, the Source of Peace, the Inspirer of Faith, the Guardian, the Victorious, the Compeller, the Greatest, the Creator, the Maker of Order, the Shaper of Beauty, the Forgiving, the Subduer, the Giver of All, the Sustainer, the Opener, the Knower of All, the Constrictor, the Reliever, the Abaser, the Exalter, the Bestower of Honors, the Humiliator, the Hearer of All, the Seer of All, the Judge, the Just, the Subtle One, the All-Aware, the Forbearing, the Magnificent, the Forgiver and Hider of Faults, the Rewarder of Thankfulness, the Highest, the Greatest, the Preserver, the

Nourisher, the Accounter, the Mighty, the Generous, the Watchful One, the Responder to Prayer, the All-Comprehending, the Perfectly Wise, the Loving One, the Majestic One, the Resurrector, the Witness, the Truth, the Trustee, the Possessor of All Strength, the Forceful One, the Governor, the Praised One, the Appraiser, the Originator, the Restorer, the Giver of Life, the Taker of Life, the Ever Living One, the Self-Existing One, the Finder, the Glorious, the Only One, the One, the Satisfier of All Needs, the All Powerful, the Creator of All Power, the Expediter, the Delayer, the First, the Last, the Manifest One, the Hidden One, the Protecting Friend, the Supreme One, the Doer of Good, the Guide to Repentance, the Avenger, the Forgiver, the Clement, the Owner of All, the Lord of Majesty and Bounty, the Equitable One, the Gatherer, the Rich One, the Enricher, the Preventer of Harm, the Creator of the Harmful, the Creator of Good, the Light, the Guide, the Originator, the Everlasting One, the Inheritor of All, the Righteous Teacher, the Patient One.

Talk Story

> Prayer is not simply getting things from God,
> that is a most initial form of prayer; prayer is
> getting into perfect communion with God.
> —*Oswald Chambers*

Have you ever heard the expression "talk story"? It is a traditional Hawaiian phrase meaning "relaxed conversation." When I lived in Hawaii, friends would gather, and we would "talk story," that is, we would chat informally, telling each other about what was going on in our lives and the lives of our family and friends. We did not speak about the weather or about flowers; rather, we spoke about what was really in our hearts, and our sharing brought a level of intimacy to our relationships. It is the same with personal prayers. Through prayer, we can reveal to God what is in our hearts and foster a level of intimacy with the Divine. To walk with the Holy is to be in conversation.

But coming to be comfortable in using our own words in prayer is always a process. As every would-be artist knows, it takes time to break out of the mold into which we were cast by our tradition before we can feel comfortable with our own expression.

I think of one of my community sisters, Paula Matthew, who is a gifted sculptor. When she was a child, every day after school her father would give her a drawing assignment of something to copy. He started out with very small things, and as her copying skill grew, so did his expectations of what she could copy. He trained her eye to see exactly what was there. At first, she had to look carefully and concentrate on her hand as she drew. As she learned to trust her hand, she could keep her eye on the object she was copying. Eventually, her ability grew to the point where she could copy whatever was put in front of her. However, Paula did very little of her own drawing because her trust was in her ability to copy the work of others. Then, when she was in high school, she finally broke out. From that time on, her work has been truly her own.

I think, too, of Pablo Picasso's work; his growth as an artist reveals a similar pattern. His blue period is characterized by a seemingly excessive emphasis on color, and his figures are recognizable as realistically human. As he developed his talent, he gained the freedom to move out of realism. Studying African masks helped him to move out of the known into the unknown. Today, when we think of Picasso, we think of "modern" pictures that abstract the essence of the human body or the essence of war; we do not think of "realistic" portraits.

Picasso described this shift as returning to the eye of a child. I see this "eye of a child" with my grandnieces, Abigail and Elizabeth. They are free with shape and color. They are not restricted to lines and what ought to be. They don't fear making mistakes or not doing it "right."

When it comes to prayer, we need to see with a child's eyes. We may not understand prayer (who does?), we may not have the "correct" words, we may not even be comfortable with praying! But the bottom line is that it is not *studying* about how to pray that leads us to the Holy, but actually *praying* that unites us with it.

I love Anthony de Mello's story of "The Explorer," from *The Song of the Bird*, because it exposes the foibles of becoming overly fascinated with knowledge.

The Explorer

The explorer returned to [her] people, who were eager to know about the Amazon. But how could [she] ever put into words the feelings that flooded [her] heart when [she] saw exotic flowers and heard the night-sounds of the forest; when [she] sensed the danger of wild beasts or paddled [her] canoe over treacherous rapids?

[She] said, "Go and find out for yourselves." To guide them [she] drew a map of the river. They pounced upon the map. They framed it in their town hall. They made copies of it for themselves. And all who had a copy considered themselves experts on the river, for did they not know its every turn and bend, how broad it was and how deep, where the rapids were and where the falls?[2]

If our prayer is only an intellectual pursuit, it's a little like pointing out the moon and then studying our finger. In other words, to learn about prayer, we need to pray.

One common area that many people seem to struggle with, when it comes to praying, is the whole idea of requesting something of God, directly: "Can I really *ask* God for something? Will my prayer really make a difference?" My response to this question is intimately tied up with the concept of free will, which I believe is one of God's great gifts to us. Because we do have free will, then the Holy must wait for us to ask.

It's a little like "tough love." Parents get into trouble if they give their children everything they think their children need. While this is necessary when children are very young, learning to be a parent means learning when to stop anticipating and letting children take the initiative.

In much the same way, I believe we need to take the initiative with God, that we need to exercise our free choice. If we want something from God, we need to have the intention and ask it of both ourselves and the Divine. This complements what Saint Augustine said: "Pray as though everything depended on God. Work as though everything depended on you."

But the issue of asking inevitably leads to the even stickier question, "What if I don't get what I ask for?" One of the wisdoms that comes with age is the realization that the shape and timing of answers may be not what we expected.

One of my mentors, Alice Edwards, would tell me that she used to pray for what she wanted, until the day she actually got it. From that point on, she began to pray for what she needed. Her belief was that God knew much better than she did what was good for her. "But," she would remind me, "you must ask."

To this, I would add one important caveat: Be clear about what you are actually asking! For years I prayed to be able to live "on the water." By "water," I meant the ocean. In the early nineties, I moved into an apartment overlooking Lake Michigan, and I realized that indeed my prayers had been answered. But now I am much more specific when I pray! My example is lighthearted, but it's important to be clear. We need to be aware of what we are really asking so we can be open to receiving a response. If we are not aware of what we are truly asking, we may not recognize God's answer.

In her book *Traveling Mercies*, Anne Lamott writes that there are really only two types of prayer: help and thank you. Whether you're an experienced pray-er or a novice, this is a great place to begin. In the end, I turn to Meister Eckhart, the Christian mystic of the fourteenth century, who said, "If the only prayer you said in your whole life was 'thank you,' that would suffice." But with intention, honesty, and a little courage, you can go much further in your communication with the Divine.

A Creating Prayer Exercise

Use Ann Lamott's succinct approach to prayer—help and thank you—to create your own prayer. Think of three people for whom you are thankful. Name each one and say specifically what you appreciate about her or him.

Then name three areas where you could use some help—either for yourself or for one of the people you've named. Be bold in your asking.

Conclude your prayer with another thank you, this time thanking the Creator for hearing you and for answering your prayer. Spend a few more moments in quiet listening for what the Divine Voice might say to you.

There Are No Boundaries

If God said,

"Rumi, pay homage to everything that has helped
  you enter my arms,"
there would not be one experience of my life,
not one thought,
not one feeling,
not any act,
I would not bow to.

—*Rumi*

It is possible that we do not recognize the prayer that is in our lives.

I have a friend who says she does not pray. What she does do, every day, is hold babies who have been abandoned. She touches them into life. She sits still and is totally present to the baby. Or she rocks and sings lullabies. She calls it her sacred duty. I call it prayer.

Another friend tells me he is not interested in a spiritual life, but he gardens in a way that cherishes the earth. He shares his produce with those less fortunate. He donates a large percentage of his money to charities. He is involved in political processes to heal the earth. He calls it his civic duty. I call it prayer.

Another companion refers to herself as totally secular. "Nothing spiritual about me," she quips. Yet people flock to her table to be fed with her culinary artistry, her humor, and the conversations that emerge from each gathering. To be in her presence is a blessing. She calls it a party. I call it a prayer.

I've heard of a woman who bakes bread as her form of prayer. She says that the process of kneading and waiting for the dough to rise, then punching it down only to knead it and let it rise again, creates a calmness in her that can only be considered prayer because during those moments she can't imagine being any closer to God.

Perhaps you have a personal practice that is outside what your faith tradition considers prayer, and therefore you do not recognize it as such. But, for you, it is communication with the Holy. I don't think the question is whether or not we pray, but what we *recognize* as what constitutes prayer. I say this because I believe prayer is in our nature.

As I write this chapter, fall is quickly approaching. The leaves in Massachusetts have started to turn, and the geese have already begun their journey to the South, as have the monarch butterflies. It is instinctual for them, in the same way I believe prayer is instinctual for us. It is in our nature to reach beyond ourselves to a greater mystery. In fact, I would go so far as to say that it is not possible for the life of a spiritual person to be devoid of communication with the sacred. There is a story in the book *The Magic Monastery* by historian Indries Shah that captures the essence of prayer as part of our persona:

In Our Nature

A cat said to a squirrel: "How wonderful it is that you can so unerringly locate buried nuts, to nurture you through the winter!"

The squirrel said: "What, to a squirrel, would be remarkable, would be a squirrel who was *unable* to do such things."[3]

I also think we naturally gravitate toward places where we feel close to God, places where we pray—and they aren't always in a church or a synagogue or a mosque or a temple. When architect Frank Lloyd Wright was asked whether he practiced any religion, he replied that he belonged to the church of Nature, with a capital N. For many of us, being outdoors, in nature, is where we feel closest to God. The might and power of storms, the swaying of prairie grasses, the breath of rivers, the trickle of streams, the vista on mountaintops, the silence of deep forests, the song of crickets, and the roar of oceans brings us to awe.

For me, the absolutely best place in nature is by water. A pond, a river, or even a creek will do, but my favorite is the ocean. Before I made my final vows, I went on a thirty-day retreat at a Franciscan monastery located near the ocean in Rye Beach, New Hampshire. Every morning, I packed my bag and strolled down to the ocean, and there, by the water, I prayed and prepared to make a lifelong commitment. The immensity of the ocean, the beauty of my surroundings, the crashing surf, and the enormous rocks became my companions for this life-giving moment of choice. That month, alone with the sea, has always been a touchstone for me.

For others, different aspects of nature call to them. My sister once told me that, during a particularly difficult time in her life, she would go out onto the porch and simply gaze at the trees. And I can't help but think of Kathy, a treasureable friend, who told me about her concept of "nurturing golf." Whenever we spend time outdoors, in whatever part of nature calls to us, we are indeed in the temple that the Creator made.

Larry Rosenberg, a meditation teacher, made a pilgrimage to holy sites in Korea. One site promised the most beautiful Buddha in all of Korea. He climbed the hill until he reached the top. The view was magnificent, but there was only a simple stone pagoda, much like pagodas he had seen before. There was no statue of the Buddha, only an empty altar—and the breathtaking view beyond. Beside the altar he read, "If you can't see the Buddha here, you had better go down and practice some more."[4]

Contemplating the Divine in the magnificent may be relatively easy, and more so, with a little practice. But what about meeting the Divine in the everyday? Yet if we are truly open to hearing the sacred, no place is out-of-bounds.

I love the traditional Jewish blessing said after using the bathroom! In our house in Alabama, we had a copy written in calligraphy on our bathroom wall so that each time we and our guests used the facilities, we could give thanks for the complexity of the human body. It reminds me not to take anything for granted.

> Blessed are You, Hashem, our God, King of the universe, Who formed us with wisdom and created within us many openings and many hollows (cavities). It is obvious and known before Your Throne of Glory that if but one of them were to be ruptured or if one of them were to be blocked it would be impossible to survive and to stand before You (even for a short period of time). Blessed are You, Hashem, Who heals all flesh and acts wondrously.

Even something as mundane as getting out of bed in the morning is grounds for prayer, as Sister Rosaline shared in one of her favorite prayers:

> *Dear God,*
> *So far today I'm doing all right.*
> *I haven't gossiped, lost my temper, been greedy,*
> *Grumpy, nasty, selfish or overindulgent.*
> *However, I'm going to get out of bed in a few minutes,*
> *And I'll need a lot of help after that. Amen.*

Personally, I have several prayers that I use quite often. When I am searching for a parking space in downtown Boston, I hold my thumb, forefinger, and middle finger together and say, "Please find me a parking space." When I am making one of my thousand-and-one requests, I pray, "Dear God, I don't ask for much (which is not quite true, but I boldly ask on); please may I have …" I also love the grace before meals that goes "Rub-a-dub-dub. Thanks, God, for the grub."

Just as there is no place out-of-bounds for prayer, there is no subject out-of-bounds. I think of the process of aging, which is ultimately a process of preparing to enter a place without boundaries. It is the most important trip of our lives and, for many of us, the scariest trip, for no one can go with us; it is a journey that we must make alone. Every letting go in our life prepares us for this final letting go. It is a final act of prayer.

My friend Nancy's mom kept this prayer about aging, attributed to an anonymous seventeenth-century nun, under glass on her dresser.

O Source of All Life, You know better than I know myself that I am growing older and will someday be old. Keep me from the fatal habit of thinking I must say something on every subject and on every occasion. Release me from craving to straighten out everybody's affairs. Make me thoughtful but not moody; helpful but not bossy. With my vast store of wisdom, it seems a pity not to use it all; but You know that I want a few friends in the end.

Keep my mind free from the recital of endless details; give me wings to get to the point. Seal my lips on my aches and pains; they are increasing, and love of rehearsing them is becoming sweeter as the years go by. I dare not ask for grace enough to enjoy the tales of others' pains, but help me to endure them with patience.

I dare not ask for improved memory, but for a growing humility, and a lessening cock-sureness when my memory seems to clash with the memories of others. Teach me the glorious lesson that occasionally I may be mistaken.

Keep me reasonably sweet: I do not want to be a saint—some of them are so very hard to live with. Give me the ability to see good things in unexpected people and give me the grace to tell them so! Amen.

A Buddhist master was once asked how much time his monks spent in prayer. "Prayer," he answered, "they spend little time in prayer. When they chop wood, they chop wood and when they carry water, they carry water." In other words, they aim to be totally present to whatever activity they are doing. Perhaps you've experienced something like this when you've been with children you love. I know that when I care for my grand-nieces, I am totally present to them. My mind does not wander, I do not long to be doing something else, and my time with them seems to fly.

And this, I believe, is what turns ordinary activities into prayer: To truly *live* in the moment, to be fully aware and present, is to be in living prayer.

A "No Boundaries" Prayer Exercise

Choose an activity that you do daily, such as making a bed, emptying trash, washing dishes, weeding in your garden, or shoveling snow. Be totally present to the activity. Be aware of every aspect of the task. When you find your mind wandering, bring it back to the activity at hand. You might repeat the words *Be Here Now* to help keep your focus. Let your total presence to the task become your prayer.

Living Prayer

> I believe that God prays in us and through us, whether we are praying
> or not (and whether we believe in God or not). So, any prayer on my
> part is a conscious response to what God is already doing in my life.
>
> —*Malcolm Boyd*

The culminating secret of prayer is summed up in the Hebrew scripture text of Micah 6:8: "And what does the Lord require of you? To act justly, and to love tenderly, and to walk humbly with your God." The three principles inherent in the universe are all contained in this one comprehensive statement.

To walk humbly with your God is to understand not only that the Holy is the one in charge of the universe, that we do not need to be in control, but also that the Holy is present within us. In describing the "interiority" principle of the universe, Thomas Berry wrote, "We bear the universe in our beings as the universe bears us in its being." At the most basic level, this is to honor the sacred in us, to know and love ourselves, to respect our integrity, and to live out our beliefs. Each one of us has a part in the greater universe, and each part matters. Each of us, and every one of our prayers, is important to the whole. When we are being the best self that we can be, not trying to be anything else, then we contribute to the whole.

To love tenderly means not only to love ourselves but also to love the other, the one who is different from us. To love tenderly is to have compassion with ourselves and let that compassion open us to feel with others. To love tenderly is to be a blessing for all with whom we come in contact. It is to honor the principle of "differentiation" and embrace the diversity of the world, its people, and the vast array of religious traditions and prayers.

To act justly is to create a world where all can coexist. To act justly is to be fair with ourselves, and others, and together repair damage where it exists. To act justly is to recognize that we are all connected, and that what each of us does—and prays—has an effect on the whole creation. To act justly is not just to talk *about* or *be* with the Divine; it is to become cocreators with the energy that creates. This is at the core of what Berry calls the "communion" principle of the universe. To act justly is to understand the need for everything to be its best self, to rejoice in the variety that composes the whole, and to heal what is not yet whole. This is what the Divine requires of all of us.

And this is the final secret of prayer: To pray is to live fully, and to live fully is to be in prayer—in motion and in stillness, in words and in gestures, in sound and in silence, in asking and in listening, in solitude and in community. Through prayer, we align ourselves with the sacred. In communicating, and listening to, and being with the one who seeks us, we participate with the numinous mystery that created life and is life itself.

There is another, interior kind of prayer ... namely, the desire of the heart.... The constancy of your desire will itself be the ceaseless voice of your prayer.

—*Augustine of Hippo*

NOTES

Secret 1: There Are Multiple Ways of Experiencing the Holy

1. Cynthia Bourgeault, *Centering Prayer and Inner Awakening* (Cambridge, MA: Cowley Publications, 2004), 31–32.

Secret 2: Your Body Is a Source of Energy for Prayer

1. Nancy Malone, *Walking a Literary Labyrinth: A Spirituality of Reading* (New York: Riverhead Books, 2003), 3–4.

2. Richard J. Foster, *Celebration of Discipline: The Path to Spiritual Growth* (San Francisco: HarperSanFrancisco, 1998).

Secret 3: Your Senses Are Vehicles of Prayer

1. Malone, *Walking a Literary Labyrinth*, 3–4.

2. Mary Margaret Funk, *Thoughts Matter: The Practice of the Spiritual Life* (New York: Continuum, 2003), 138.

3. Dr. George Washington Carver, as quoted by Peter Tompkins and Christopher Bird in *The Secret Life of Plants* (New York: Harper Collins, 2002), 136–41.

4. Teresa of Ávila, as quoted by Victoria Lincoln in *Teresa: A Woman* (Albany: State University of New York Press, 1994), 63.

Secret 4: Diversity Nourishes Prayer

1. Louise Hay, "Deep at the center of my being," from *You Can Heal Your Life* (Carlsbad, CA: Hay House, 1984), 206.

2. *Oxford Book of Prayer* (New York: Oxford University Press, 2002), 112.

3. English translation of the Kaddish from Congregation Beth El's (Sudbury River Valley, Sudbury, MA) prayer book, *Vetaher Libenu*.

4. Pema Chödrön, *The Places That Scare You: A Guide to Fearlessness in Difficult Times* (Boston: Shambhala Publications, 2001), 37.

5. Macrina Wiederkehr, "Final Blessing," from *The Song of the Seed: A Monastic Way of Tending the Soul* (New York: HarperCollins, 1995), 139.

6. Neil Douglas-Klotz, "O Thou, the Breath, the Light of All," from *Prayers of the Cosmos: Meditations on the Aramaic Words of Jesus* (New York: HarperCollins, 1994), 41.

7. Prayer by Mychal Judge. The Holy Name Province, Order of Friars Minor.

Secret 5: Interconnectedness Gives Prayer Life

1. Invocation given by Dr. Ingrid L. Schafer at the 86th annual technical meeting of the Oklahoma Academy of Science, University of Science and Arts of Oklahoma, November 7, 1997.

2. Brian Swimme, *The Universe Is a Green Dragon: A Cosmic Creation Story* (Santa Fe: Bear, 1985), 43.

3. Etty Hillesum, as quoted by Carol Lee Flinders in *Enduring Lives: Portraits of Women and Faith in Action* (New York: Jeremy P. Tarcher/Penguin, 2006), 69.

4. Anthony de Mello, "Shout to Keep Safe—And Certain," from *The Song of the Bird* (New York: Doubleday, 1984), 59.

5. Ann Weems, from *Kneeling in Jerusalem* (Louisville, KY: Westminster/John Knox Press, 1993), 28.

6. Dorothee Soelle, *The Silent Cry: Mysticism and Resistance,* trans. Barbara and Martin Rumscheidt (Minneapolis: Augsburg Fortress Press, 2001).

7. de Mello, "The Monk and the Woman," from *The Song of the Bird*, 108–9.

Secret 6: To Learn about Prayer, You Need to Pray

1. Joyce Rupp, *Prayers to Sophia* (Notre Dame, IN: Ave Maria Press, 2000), 14.

2. de Mello, "The Explorer," from *The Song of the Bird*, 32–33.

3. Indries Shah, *The Magic Monastery: Analogical and Action Philosophy of the Middle East and Central Asia* (London: Cape, 1972), 41.

4. Larry Rosenberg, as quoted by Jack Kornfield in *After the Ecstasy, the Laundry: How the Heart Grows Wise on the Spiritual Path* (New York: Bantam Books, 2000), 105–6.

SUGGESTIONS FOR FURTHER READING

Cahill, Thomas. *The Gifts of the Jews: How a Tribe of Desert Nomads Changed the Way Everyone Thinks and Feels*. New York: Doubleday, 1998.

Cooper, Rabbi David A. *God Is a Verb: Kabbalah and the Practice of Mystical Judaism*. New York: Riverhead Books, 1997.

de Mello, Anthony. *One Minute Nonsense*. Chicago: Loyola University Press, 1992.

———. *One Minute Wisdom*. New York: Doubleday, 1986.

———. *The Song of the Bird*. New York: Doubleday, 1984.

———. *Taking Flight: A Book of Story Meditations*. New York: Doubleday, 1988.

Dosick, Rabbi Wayne. *Dancing with God: Everyday Steps to Jewish Spiritual Renewal*. San Francisco: HarperSanFrancisco, 1997.

Douglas-Klotz, Neil. *Prayers of the Cosmos: Meditations on the Aramaic Words of Jesus*. San Francisco: HarperSanFrancisco, 1994.

Finley, Mitch. *Prayer for People Who Think Too Much: A Guide to Everyday, Anywhere Prayer from the World's Faith Traditions*. Woodstock, VT: SkyLight Paths Publishing, 1999.

Furlong, Monica, ed. *Women Pray: Voices through the Ages from Many Faiths, Cultures and Traditions*. Woodstock, VT: SkyLight Paths Publishing, 2001.

Griffin, Emilie. *Doors into Prayer: An Invitation*. Brewster, MA: Paraclete Press, 2001.

Henry, Gray, and Susannah Marriott. *Beads of Faith: Pathways to Meditation and Spirituality Using Rosaries, Prayer Beads and Sacred Words*. London: Carroll & Brown, 2002.

Jackson, Christal, ed. *Women of Color Pray: Voices of Strength, Faith, Healing, Hope and Courage*. Woodstock, VT: SkyLight Paths Publishing: 2005.

Johnston, William. *Silent Music: The Science of Meditation.* New York: Fordham University Press, 1997.

Kornfield, Jack. *After the Ecstasy, the Laundry: How the Heart Grows Wise on the Spiritual Path.* New York: Bantam Books, 2000.

Ladinsky, Daniel. *Love Poems from God: Twelve Sacred Voices from the East and West.* New York: Penguin Compass, 2002.

Ochs, Carol, and Kerry M. Olitzky. *Jewish Spiritual Guidance: Finding Our Way to God.* San Francisco: Jossey-Bass, 1997.

Pennington, M. Basil. *Centering Prayer: Renewing an Ancient Christian Prayer Form.* New York: Doubleday, 1980.

Pennington, M. Basil, Thomas Keating, and Thomas E. Clarke. *Finding Grace at the Center: The Beginning of Centering Prayer.* 3rd ed. Woodstock, VT: SkyLight Paths Publishing, 2006.

Silf, Margaret. *The Gift of Prayer: Embracing the Sacred in the Everyday.* New York: Blue Bridge, 2004.

Smith, Huston. *The World's Religions: Our Great Wisdom Traditions.* San Francisco: HarperSanFrancisco, 1991.

Soelle, Dorothee. *The Silent Cry: Mysticism and Resistance.* Translated by Barbara and Martin Rumscheidt. Minneapolis: Augsburg Fortress Press, 2001.

Sweeney, Jon M. *Praying with Our Hands: 21 Practices of Embodied Prayer from the World's Spiritual Traditions.* Woodstock, VT: SkyLight Paths Publishing, 2000.

CREDITS

The author is grateful for permission to reprint the following copyrighted material:

"The Great Invocation" (Adapted Version) by Alice Bailey. Reprinted by permission of Lucis Trust.

"The Explorer," "The Monk and the Woman," "Shout to Keep Safe—And Certain" from *The Song of the Bird* by Anthony de Mello. Copyright © 1982, 1984 by Anthony de Mello, S. J. Used by permission of Doubleday, a division of Random House, Inc.

"O Thou, the Breath, the Light of All" (14 lines) from *Prayers of the Cosmos: Meditations on the Aramaic Words of Jesus* by Neil Douglas-Klotz. Copyright © 1990 by Neil Douglas-Klotz. Reprinted by permission of HarperCollins Publishers.

"Deep at the center of my being" from *You Can Heal Your Life* by Louise Hay. Reprinted by permission of Hay House, Inc., Carlsbad, CA.

Prayer by Mychal Judge. Reprinted by permission of the Holy Name Province, Order of Friars Minor.

English translation of the Kaddish from Congregation Beth El's prayer book, *Vetaher Libenu*, reprinted by permission of the Congregation Beth El of the Sudbury River Valley, Sudbury, MA.

"In Memory" by Dr. Ingrid L. Schafer. Reprinted by permission of the author.

"We Pray This Day" from *Kneeling in Jerusalem* by Ann Weems. Copyright © 1987 by Ann Weems. Used by permission of Westminster John Knox Press.

"Final Blessing" (seven lines) from *The Song of the Seed* by Macrina Wiederkehr. Copyright © 1995 by Macrina Wiederkehr. Reprinted by permission of HarperCollins Publishers.

Every effort has been made to obtain the necessary permissions to use copyrighted material. If any material has been unintentionally used without proper permission, please contact the author so that appropriate credit is acknowledged in future editions.

ACKNOWLEDGMENTS

I am so very grateful:

to the Angel-in-Purple on the beach in Maine for having the courage to speak to a skeptic;

to my editors Emily Wichland, Maura D. Shaw, and Marcia Broucek, whose knowledge, questions, challenges, and endless work on my behalf make me appear a clear and articulate writer;

to my sister, Julie Krasker, and my brother, James Corcoran, who rose to the occasion when I needed space;

to Nancy L. Hennessey for her offer of solace, solitude, and wonderful companionship when I really needed to get away to write;

to Ada Maria Isasi-Diaz, Sherrin Langeler, Anne Leslie, and Jane Tedder for gifts of invaluable sources;

to Barcy Fox and Joani Mountain, who made sure I had the semblance of a social life in the midst of a writer's isolation;

to Joan Filla, who listened to every chapter via long distance and proposed creative directions for the work;

to the Women of Wisdom from the Salons, RUAH, St. Julia and St. Mary's, the Ladies of Light, and *grass/roots* council members, who put up with my groans, rants, rages, and absences;

finally, my gratitude to my mother, Helen Warren Corcoran, who always believed I had a book in me.

Global Spiritual Perspectives

Spiritual Perspectives on America's Role as Superpower
by the Editors at SkyLight Paths

Are we the world's good neighbor or a global bully? From a spiritual perspective, what are America's responsibilities as the only remaining superpower? Contributors:

Dr. Beatrice Bruteau • Dr. Joan Brown Campbell • Tony Campolo • Rev. Forrest Church • Lama Surya Das • Matthew Fox • Kabir Helminski • Thich Nhat Hanh • Eboo Patel • Abbot M. Basil Pennington, ocso • Dennis Prager • Rosemary Radford Ruether • Wayne Teasdale • Rev. William McD. Tully • Rabbi Arthur Waskow • John Wilson

5½ x 8½, 256 pp, Quality PB, 978-1-893361-81-2 **$16.95**

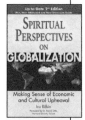

Spiritual Perspectives on Globalization, 2nd Edition
Making Sense of Economic and Cultural Upheaval
by Ira Rifkin; Foreword by Dr. David Little, Harvard Divinity School

What is globalization? Surveys the religious landscape. Includes a new Discussion Guide designed for group use.

5½ x 8½, 256 pp, Quality PB, 978-1-59473-045-0 **$16.99**

Hinduism / Vedanta

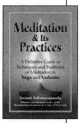

The Four Yogas
A Guide to the Spiritual Paths of Action, Devotion, Meditation and Knowledge
by Swami Adiswarananda 6 x 9, 320 pp, HC, 978-1-59473-143-3 **$29.99**

Meditation & Its Practices
A Definitive Guide to Techniques and Traditions of Meditation in Yoga and Vedanta
by Swami Adiswarananda 6 x 9, 504 pp, Quality PB, 978-1-59473-105-1 **$19.99**

The Spiritual Quest and the Way of Yoga: The Goal, the Journey and the Milestones
by Swami Adiswarananda 6 x 9, 288 pp, HC, 978-1-59473-113-6 **$29.99**

Sri Ramakrishna, the Face of Silence
by Swami Nikhilananda and Dhan Gopal Mukerji
Edited with an Introduction by Swami Adiswarananda; Foreword by Dhan Gopal Mukerji II
Classic biographies present the life and thought of Sri Ramakrishna.
6 x 9, 352 pp, HC, 978-1-59473-115-0 **$29.99**

Sri Sarada Devi, The Holy Mother
Her Teachings and Conversations
Translated with Notes by Swami Nikhilananda; Edited with an Introduction by Swami Adiswarananda
6 x 9, 288 pp, HC, 978-1-59473-070-2 **$29.99**

The Vedanta Way to Peace and Happiness *by Swami Adiswarananda*
6 x 9, 240 pp, HC, 978-1-59473-034-4 **$29.99**

Vivekananda, World Teacher: His Teachings on the Spiritual Unity of Humankind
Edited and with an Introduction by Swami Adiswarananda
6 x 9, 272 pp, Quality PB, 978-1-59473-210-2 **$21.99**

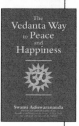

Sikhism

The First Sikh Spiritual Master
Timeless Wisdom from the Life and Teachings of Guru Nanak *by Harish Dhillon*
Tells the story of a unique spiritual leader who showed a gentle, peaceful path to God-realization while highlighting Guru Nanak's quest for tolerance and compassion. 6 x 9, 192 pp, Quality PB, 978-1-59473-209-6 **$16.99**

Or phone, fax, mail or e-mail to: **SKYLIGHT PATHS** Publishing
Sunset Farm Offices, Route 4 • P.O. Box 237 • Woodstock, Vermont 05091
Tel: (802) 457-4000 • Fax: (802) 457-4004 • www.skylightpaths.com
Credit card orders: **(800) 962-4544** (8:30AM–5:30PM ET Monday–Friday)
Generous discounts on quantity orders. SATISFACTION GUARANTEED. Prices subject to change.

Sacred Texts—SkyLight Illuminations Series

Offers today's spiritual seeker an accessible entry into the great classic texts of the world's spiritual traditions. Each classic is presented in an accessible translation, with facing pages of guided commentary from experts, giving you the keys you need to understand the history, context and meaning of the text. This series enables you, whatever your background, to experience and understand classic spiritual texts directly, and to make them a part of your life.

CHRISTIANITY

The End of Days: Essential Selections from Apocalyptic Texts—
Annotated & Explained   *Annotation by Robert G. Clouse*
Helps you understand the complex Christian visions of the end of the world.
5½ x 8½, 224 pp, Quality PB, 978-1-59473-170-9 **$16.99**

The Hidden Gospel of Matthew: Annotated & Explained
Translation & Annotation by Ron Miller
Takes you deep into the text cherished around the world to discover the words and events that have the strongest connection to the historical Jesus.
5½ x 8½, 272 pp, Quality PB, 978-1-59473-038-2 **$16.99**

The Lost Sayings of Jesus: Teachings from Ancient Christian, Jewish,
Gnostic and Islamic Sources—Annotated & Explained
Translation & Annotation by Andrew Phillip Smith; Foreword by Stephan A. Hoeller
This collection of more than three hundred sayings depicts Jesus as a Wisdom teacher who speaks to people of all faiths as a mystic and spiritual master.
5½ x 8½, 240 pp, Quality PB, 978-1-59473-172-3 **$16.99**

Philokalia: The Eastern Christian Spiritual Texts—Selections Annotated &
Explained   *Annotation by Allyne Smith; Translation by G. E. H. Palmer, Phillip Sherrard and Bishop Kallistos Ware*
The first approachable introduction to the wisdom of the Philokalia, which is the classic text of Eastern Christian spirituality.
5½ x 8½, 240 pp, Quality PB, 978-1-59473-103-7 **$16.99**

Spiritual Writings on Mary: Annotated & Explained
Annotation by Mary Ford-Grabowsky; Foreword by Andrew Harvey
Examines the role of Mary, the mother of Jesus, as a source of inspiration in history and in life today.   5½ x 8½, 288 pp, Quality PB, 978-1-59473-001-6 **$16.99**

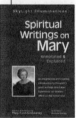

The Way of a Pilgrim: Annotated & Explained
Translation & Annotation by Gleb Pokrovsky; Foreword by Andrew Harvey
This classic of Russian spirituality is the delightful account of one man who sets out to learn the prayer of the heart, also known as the "Jesus prayer."
5½ x 8½, 160 pp, Illus., Quality PB, 978-1-893361-31-7 **$14.95**

MORMONISM

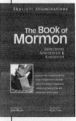

The Book of Mormon: Selections Annotated & Explained
Annotation by Jana Riess; Foreword by Phyllis Tickle
Explores the sacred epic that is cherished by more than twelve million members of the LDS church as the keystone of their faith.
5½ x 8½ , 272 pp, Quality PB, 978-1-59473-076-4 **$16.99**

NATIVE AMERICAN

Native American Stories of the Sacred: Annotated & Explained
Retold & Annotated by Evan T. Pritchard
Intended for more than entertainment, these teaching tales contain elegantly simple illustrations of time-honored truths.
5½ x 8½, 272 pp, Quality PB, 978-1-59473-112-9 **$16.99**

Sacred Texts—cont.

GNOSTICISM

The Gospel of Philip: Annotated & Explained
Translation & Annotation by Andrew Phillip Smith; Foreword by Stevan Davies
Reveals otherwise unrecorded sayings of Jesus and fragments of Gnostic mythology.
5½ x 8½, 160 pp, Quality PB, 978-1-59473-111-2 **$16.99**

The Gospel of Thomas: Annotated & Explained
Translation & Annotation by Stevan Davies Sheds new light on the origins of Christianity and portrays Jesus as a wisdom-loving sage. 5½ x 8½, 192 pp, Quality PB, 978-1-893361-45-4 **$16.99**

The Secret Book of John: The Gnostic Gospel—Annotated & Explained
Translation & Annotation by Stevan Davies The most significant and influential text of the ancient Gnostic religion. 5½ x 8½, 208 pp, Quality PB, 978-1-59473-082-5 **$16.99**

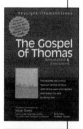

JUDAISM

The Divine Feminine in Biblical Wisdom Literature
Selections Annotated & Explained
Translation & Annotation by Rabbi Rami Shapiro; Foreword by Rev. Cynthia Bourgeault, PhD
Uses the Hebrew books of Psalms, Proverbs, Song of Songs, Ecclesiastes and Job, Wisdom literature and the Wisdom of Solomon to clarify who Wisdom is.
5½ x 8½, 240 pp, Quality PB, 978-1-59473-109-9 **$16.99**

Ethics of the Sages: *Pirke Avot*—Annotated & Explained
Translation & Annotation by Rabbi Rami Shapiro Clarifies the ethical teachings of the early Rabbis. 5½ x 8½, 192 pp, Quality PB, 978-1-59473-207-2 **$16.99**

Hasidic Tales: Annotated & Explained
Translation & Annotation by Rabbi Rami Shapiro
Introduces the legendary tales of the impassioned Hasidic rabbis, presenting them as stories rather than as parables. 5½ x 8½, 240 pp, Quality PB, 978-1-893361-86-7 **$16.95**

The Hebrew Prophets: Selections Annotated & Explained
Translation & Annotation by Rabbi Rami Shapiro; Foreword by Zalman M. Schachter-Shalomi
Focuses on the central themes covered by all the Hebrew prophets.
5½ x 8½, 224 pp, Quality PB, 978-1-59473-037-5 **$16.99**

Zohar: Annotated & Explained *Translation & Annotation by Daniel C. Matt*
The best-selling author of *The Essential Kabbalah* brings together in one place the most important teachings of the Zohar, the canonical text of Jewish mystical tradition.
5½ x 8½, 176 pp, Quality PB, 978-1-893361-51-5 **$15.99**

EASTERN RELIGIONS

Bhagavad Gita: Annotated & Explained *Translation by Shri Purohit Swami*
Annotation by Kendra Crossen Burroughs Explains references and philosophical terms, shares the interpretations of famous spiritual leaders and scholars, and more.
5½ x 8½, 192 pp, Quality PB, 978-1-893361-28-7 **$16.95**

Dhammapada: Annotated & Explained *Translation by Max Müller and revised by Jack Maguire; Annotation by Jack Maguire* Contains all of Buddhism's key teachings.
5½ x 8½, 160 pp, b/w photos, Quality PB, 978-1-893361-42-3 **$14.95**

Rumi and Islam: Selections from His Stories, Poems, and Discourses—
Annotated & Explained *Translation & Annotation by Ibrahim Gamard*
Focuses on Rumi's place within the Sufi tradition of Islam, providing insight into the mystical side of the religion. 5½ x 8½, 240 pp, Quality PB, 978-1-59473-002-3 **$15.99**

Selections from the Gospel of Sri Ramakrishna: Annotated & Explained
Translation by Swami Nikhilananda; Annotation by Kendra Crossen Burroughs
Introduces the fascinating world of the Indian mystic and the universal appeal of his message. 5½ x 8½, 240 pp, b/w photos, Quality PB, 978-1-893361-46-1 **$16.95**

Tao Te Ching: Annotated & Explained *Translation & Annotation by Derek Lin*
Foreword by Lama Surya Das Introduces an Eastern classic in an accessible, poetic and completely original way. 5½ x 8½, 192 pp, Quality PB, 978-1-59473-204-1 **$16.99**

Spirituality

Jewish Spirituality: A Brief Introduction for Christians   by *Lawrence Kushner*
5½ x 8½, 112 pp, Quality PB, 978-1-58023-150-3 **$12.95** *(a Jewish Lights book)*

Journeys of Simplicity: Traveling Light with Thomas Merton, Bashō, Edward Abbey, Annie Dillard & Others by *Philip Harnden* 5 x 7¼, 128 pp, HC, 978-1-893361-76-8 **$16.95**

Keeping Spiritual Balance As We Grow Older: More than 65 Creative Ways to Use Purpose, Prayer, and the Power of Spirit to Build a Meaningful Retirement
by *Molly and Bernie Srode* 8 x 8, 224 pp, Quality PB, 978-1-59473-042-9 **$16.99**

The Monks of Mount Athos: A Western Monk's Extraordinary Spiritual Journey on Eastern Holy Ground by *M. Basil Pennington, ocso; Foreword by Archimandrite Dionysios*
6 x 9, 256 pp, 10+ b/w line drawings, Quality PB, 978-1-893361-78-2 **$18.95**

One God Clapping: The Spiritual Path of a Zen Rabbi by *Alan Lew with Sherril Jaffe*
5½ x 8½, 336 pp, Quality PB, 978-1-58023-115-2 **$16.95** *(a Jewish Lights book)*

Prayer for People Who Think Too Much: A Guide to Everyday, Anywhere Prayer from the World's Faith Traditions by *Mitch Finley*
5½ x 8½, 224 pp, Quality PB, 978-1-893361-21-8 **$16.99**; HC, 978-1-893361-00-3 **$21.95**

Show Me Your Way: The Complete Guide to Exploring Interfaith Spiritual Direction
by *Howard A. Addison*   5½ x 8½, 240 pp, Quality PB, 978-1-893361-41-6 **$16.95**

Spirituality 101: The Indispensable Guide to Keeping—or Finding—Your Spiritual Life on Campus by *Harriet L. Schwartz, with contributions from college students at nearly thirty campuses across the United States* 6 x 9, 272 pp, Quality PB, 978-1-59473-000-9 **$16.99**

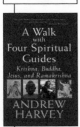

Spiritually Incorrect: Finding God in All the Wrong Places by *Dan Wakefield; Illus. by Marian DelVecchio* 5½ x 8½, 192 pp, b/w illus., Quality PB, 978-1-59473-137-2 **$15.99**

Spiritual Manifestos: Visions for Renewed Religious Life in America from Young Spiritual Leaders of Many Faiths *Edited by Niles Elliot Goldstein; Preface by Martin E. Marty*
6 x 9, 256 pp, HC, 978-1-893361-09-6 **$21.95**

A Walk with Four Spiritual Guides: Krishna, Buddha, Jesus, and Ramakrishna
by *Andrew Harvey* 5½ x 8½, 192 pp, 10 b/w photos & illus., Quality PB, 978-1-59473-138-9 **$15.99**

What Matters: Spiritual Nourishment for Head and Heart
by *Frederick Franck* 5 x 7¼, 128 pp, 50+ b/w illus., HC, 978-1-59473-013-9 **$16.99**

Who Is My God?, 2nd Edition: An Innovative Guide to Finding Your Spiritual Identity
Created by the Editors at SkyLight Paths 6 x 9, 160 pp, Quality PB, 978-1-59473-014-6 **$15.99**

Spirituality—A Week Inside

Come and Sit: A Week Inside Meditation Centers
by *Marcia Z. Nelson; Foreword by Wayne Teasdale*
The insider's guide to meditation in a variety of different spiritual traditions—Buddhist, Hindu, Christian, Jewish, and Sufi traditions.
6 x 9, 224 pp, b/w photos, Quality PB, 978-1-893361-35-5 **$16.95**

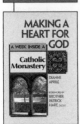

Lighting the Lamp of Wisdom: A Week Inside a Yoga Ashram
by *John Ittner; Foreword by Dr. David Frawley*
This insider's guide to Hindu spiritual life takes you into a typical week of retreat inside a yoga ashram to demystify the experience and show you what to expect.
6 x 9, 192 pp, 10+ b/w photos, Quality PB, 978-1-893361-52-2 **$15.95**

Making a Heart for God: A Week Inside a Catholic Monastery
by *Dianne Aprile; Foreword by Brother Patrick Hart, ocso*
Takes you to the Abbey of Gethsemani—the Trappist monastery in Kentucky that was home to author Thomas Merton—to explore the details.
6 x 9, 224 pp, b/w photos, Quality PB, 978-1-893361-49-2 **$16.95**

Waking Up: A Week Inside a Zen Monastery
by *Jack Maguire; Foreword by John Daido Loori, Roshi*
An essential guide to what it's like to spend a week inside a Zen Buddhist monastery.
6 x 9, 224 pp, b/w photos, Quality PB, 978-1-893361-55-3 **$16.95**
HC, 978-1-893361-13-3 **$21.95**

Spirituality of the Seasons

Autumn: A Spiritual Biography of the Season
Edited by Gary Schmidt and Susan M. Felch; Illustrations by Mary Azarian
Rejoice in autumn as a time of preparation and reflection. Includes Wendell Berry, David James Duncan, Robert Frost, A. Bartlett Giamatti, E. B. White, P. D. James, Julian of Norwich, Garret Keizer, Tracy Kidder, Anne Lamott, May Sarton.
6 x 9, 320 pp, 5 b/w illus., Quality PB, 978-1-59473-118-1 **$18.99**
HC, 978-1-59473-005-4 **$22.99**

Spring: A Spiritual Biography of the Season
Edited by Gary Schmidt and Susan M. Felch; Illustrations by Mary Azarian
Explore the gentle unfurling of spring and reflect on how nature celebrates rebirth and renewal. Includes Jane Kenyon, Lucy Larcom, Harry Thurston, Nathaniel Hawthorne, Noel Perrin, Annie Dillard, Martha Ballard, Barbara Kingsolver, Dorothy Wordsworth, Donald Hall, David Brill, Lionel Basney, Isak Dinesen, Paul Laurence Dunbar. 6 x 9, 352 pp, 6 b/w illus., HC, 978-1-59473-114-3 **$21.99**

Summer: A Spiritual Biography of the Season
Edited by Gary Schmidt and Susan M. Felch; Illustrations by Barry Moser
"A sumptuous banquet.... These selections lift up an exquisite wholeness found within an everyday sophistication."— ★ *Publishers Weekly* starred review
Includes Anne Lamott, Luci Shaw, Ray Bradbury, Richard Selzer, Thomas Lynch, Walt Whitman, Carl Sandburg, Sherman Alexie, Madeleine L'Engle, Jamaica Kincaid.
6 x 9, 304 pp, 5 b/w illus., Quality PB, 978-1-59473-183-9 **$18.99**
HC, 978-1-59473-083-2 **$21.99**

Winter: A Spiritual Biography of the Season
Edited by Gary Schmidt and Susan M. Felch; Illustrations by Barry Moser
"This outstanding anthology features top-flight nature and spirituality writers on the fierce, inexorable season of winter.... Remarkably lively and warm, despite the icy subject." — ★ *Publishers Weekly* starred review.
Includes Will Campbell, Rachel Carson, Annie Dillard, Donald Hall, Ron Hansen, Jane Kenyon, Jamaica Kincaid, Barry Lopez, Kathleen Norris, John Updike, E. B. White.
6 x 9, 288 pp, 6 b/w illus., Deluxe PB w/flaps, 978-1-893361-92-8 **$18.95**
HC, 978-1-893361-53-9 **$21.95**

Spirituality / Animal Companions

Blessing the Animals: Prayers and Ceremonies to Celebrate God's Creatures, Wild and Tame *Edited by Lynn L. Caruso* 5 x 7¼, 256 pp, HC, 978-1-59473-145-7 **$19.99**

What Animals Can Teach Us about Spirituality: Inspiring Lessons from Wild and Tame Creatures *by Diana L. Guerrero* 6 x 9, 176 pp, Quality PB, 978-1-893361-84-3 **$16.95**

Spirituality

Awakening the Spirit, Inspiring the Soul
30 Stories of Interspiritual Discovery in the Community of Faiths
Edited by Brother Wayne Teasdale and Martha Howard, MD; Foreword by Joan Borysenko, PhD
Thirty original spiritual mini-autobiographies showcase the varied ways that people come to faith—and what that means—in today's multi-religious world.
6 x 9, 224 pp, HC, 978-1-59473-039-9 **$21.99**

The Alphabet of Paradise: An A–Z of Spirituality for Everyday Life
by Howard Cooper 5 x 7¾, 224 pp, Quality PB, 978-1-893361-80-5 **$16.95**

Creating a Spiritual Retirement: A Guide to the Unseen Possibilities in Our Lives
by Molly Srode 6 x 9, 208 pp, b/w photos, Quality PB, 978-1-59473-050-4 **$14.99**
HC, 978-1-893361-75-1 **$19.95**

Finding Hope: Cultivating God's Gift of a Hopeful Spirit
by Marcia Ford 8 x 8, 200 pp, Quality PB, 978-1-59473-211-9 **$16.99**

The Geography of Faith: Underground Conversations on Religious, Political and Social Change *by Daniel Berrigan and Robert Coles* 6 x 9, 224 pp, Quality PB, 978-1-893361-40-9 **$16.95**

God Within: Our Spiritual Future—As Told by Today's New Adults *Edited by Jon M. Sweeney and the Editors at SkyLight Paths* 6 x 9, 176 pp, Quality PB, 978-1-893361-15-7 **$14.95**

Spirituality & Crafts

The Knitting Way: A Guide to Spiritual Self-Discovery
by Linda Skolnik and Janice MacDaniels
7 x 9, 240 pp, Quality PB, b/w photographs, 978-1-59473-079-5 **$16.99**

The Quilting Path: A Guide to Spiritual Discovery through Fabric, Thread and Kabbalah
by Louise Silk
7 x 9, 192 pp, Quality PB, b/w photographs and illustrations, 978-1-59473-206-5 **$16.99**

The Scrapbooking Journey: A Hands-On Guide to Spiritual Discovery
by Cory Richardson-Lauve; Foreword by Stacy Julian
7 x 9, 176 pp, Quality PB, 8-page full-color insert, plus b/w photographs
978-1-59473-216-4 **$18.99**

Spiritual Practice

Divining the Body: Reclaim the Holiness of Your Physical Self
by Jan Phillips
A practical and inspiring guidebook for connecting the body and soul in spiritual practice. Leads you into a milieu of reverence, mystery and delight, helping you discover your body as a pathway to the Divine.
8 x 8, 256 pp, Quality PB, 978-1-59473-080-1 **$16.99**

Finding Time for the Timeless: Spirituality in the Workweek
by John McQuiston II

Simple, refreshing stories that provide you with examples of how you can refocus and enrich your daily life using prayer or meditation, ritual and other forms of spiritual practice. 5½ x 6¾, 208 pp, HC, 978-1-59473-035-1 **$17.99**

The Gospel of Thomas: A Guidebook for Spiritual Practice
by Ron Miller; Translations by Stevan Davies
An innovative guide to bring a new spiritual classic into daily life.
6 x 9, 160 pp, Quality PB, 978-1-59473-047-4 **$14.99**

Earth, Water, Fire, and Air: Essential Ways of Connecting to Spirit
by Cait Johnson 6 x 9, 224 pp, HC, 978-1-893361-65-2 **$19.95**

Labyrinths from the Outside In: Walking to Spiritual Insight—A Beginner's Guide
by Donna Schaper and Carole Ann Camp
6 x 9, 208 pp, b/w illus. and photos, Quality PB, 978-1-893361-18-8 **$16.95**

Practicing the Sacred Art of Listening: A Guide to Enrich Your Relationships and Kindle Your Spiritual Life—The Listening Center Workshop
by Kay Lindahl 8 x 8, 176 pp, Quality PB, 978-1-893361-85-0 **$16.95**

Releasing the Creative Spirit: Unleash the Creativity in Your Life
by Dan Wakefield 7 x 10, 256 pp, Quality PB, 978-1-893361-36-2 **$16.95**

The Sacred Art of Bowing: Preparing to Practice
by Andi Young 5½ x 8½, 128 pp, b/w illus., Quality PB, 978-1-893361-82-9 **$14.95**

The Sacred Art of Chant: Preparing to Practice
by Ana Hernández 5½ x 8½, 192 pp, Quality PB, 978-1-59473-036-8 **$15.99**

The Sacred Art of Fasting: Preparing to Practice
by Thomas Ryan, CSP 5½ x 8½, 192 pp, Quality PB, 978-1-59473-078-8 **$15.99**

The Sacred Art of Forgiveness: Forgiving Ourselves and Others through God's Grace
by Marcia Ford 8 x 8, 176 pp, Quality PB, 978-1-59473-175-4 **$16.99**

The Sacred Art of Listening: Forty Reflections for Cultivating a Spiritual Practice
by Kay Lindahl; Illustrations by Amy Schnapper
8 x 8, 160 pp, b/w illus., Quality PB, 978-1-893361-44-7 **$16.99**

The Sacred Art of Lovingkindness: Preparing to Practice
by Rabbi Rami Shapiro; Foreword by Marcia Ford
5½ x 8½, 176 pp, Quality PB, 978-1-59473-151-8 **$16.99**

Sacred Speech: A Practical Guide for Keeping Spirit in Your Speech
by Rev. Donna Schaper 6 x 9, 176 pp, Quality PB, 978-1-59473-068-9 **$15.99**
HC, 978-1-893361-74-4 **$21.95**

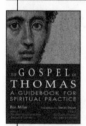

Meditation / Prayer

Prayers to an Evolutionary God
by William Cleary; Afterword by Diarmuid O'Murchu

How is it possible to pray when God is dislocated from heaven, dispersed all around us, and more of a creative force than an all-knowing father? Inspired by the spiritual and scientific teachings of Diarmuid O'Murchu and Teilhard de Chardin, Cleary reveals that religion and science can be combined to create an expanding view of the universe—an evolutionary faith.

6 x 9, 208 pp, HC, 978-1-59473-006-1 **$21.99**

Psalms: A Spiritual Commentary
by M. Basil Pennington, OCSO; Illustrations by Phillip Ratner

Showing how the Psalms give profound and candid expression to both our highest aspirations and our deepest pain, the late, highly respected Cistercian Abbot M. Basil Pennington shares his reflections on some of the most beloved passages from the Bible's most widely read book.

6 x 9, 176 pp, HC, 24 full-page b/w illus., 978-1-59473-141-9 **$19.99**

The Song of Songs: A Spiritual Commentary
by M. Basil Pennington, OCSO; Illustrations by Phillip Ratner

Join the late M. Basil Pennington as he ruminates on the Bible's most challenging mystical text. Follow a path into the Songs that weaves through his inspired words and the evocative drawings of Jewish artist Phillip Ratner—a path that reveals your own humanity and leads to the deepest delight of your soul.

6 x 9, 160 pp, HC, 14 b/w illus., 978-1-59473-004-7 **$19.99**

Women of Color Pray: Voices of Strength, Faith, Healing,
Hope and Courage *Edited and with Introductions by Christal M. Jackson*

Through these prayers, poetry, lyrics, meditations and affirmations, you will share in the strong and undeniable connection women of color share with God. It will challenge you to explore new ways of prayerful expression.

5 x 7¼, 208 pp, Quality PB, 978-1-59473-077-1 **$15.99**

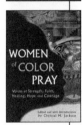

The Art of Public Prayer: Not for Clergy Only
by Lawrence A. Hoffman

An ecumenical resource for all people looking to change hardened worship patterns.

6 x 9, 288 pp, Quality PB, 978-1-893361-06-5 **$18.99**

Finding Grace at the Center, 3rd Ed.: The Beginning of Centering Prayer
by M. Basil Pennington, OCSO, Thomas Keating, OCSO, and Thomas E. Clarke, SJ
Foreword by Rev. Cynthia Bourgeault, PhD

5 x 7¼, 128 pp, Quality PB, 978-1-59473-182-2 **$12.99**

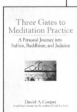

A Heart of Stillness: A Complete Guide to Learning the Art of Meditation
by David A. Cooper 5½ x 8½, 272 pp, Quality PB, 978-1-893361-03-4 **$16.95**

Meditation without Gurus: A Guide to the Heart of Practice
by Clark Strand 5½ x 8½, 192 pp, Quality PB, 978-1-893361-93-5 **$16.95**

Praying with Our Hands: 21 Practices of Embodied Prayer from the World's
Spiritual Traditions *by Jon M. Sweeney; Photographs by Jennifer J. Wilson; Foreword by Mother Tessa Bielecki; Afterword by Taitetsu Unno, PhD*

8 x 8, 96 pp, 22 duotone photos, Quality PB, 978-1-893361-16-4 **$16.95**

Silence, Simplicity & Solitude: A Complete Guide to Spiritual Retreat at Home
by David A. Cooper 5½ x 8½, 336 pp, Quality PB, 978-1-893361-04-1 **$16.95**

Three Gates to Meditation Practice: A Personal Journey into Sufism, Buddhism,
and Judaism *by David A. Cooper* 5½ x 8½, 240 pp, Quality PB, 978-1-893361-22-5 **$16.95**

Three Gates to
Meditation Practice
A Personal Journey into
Sufism, Buddhism, and Judaism

David A. Cooper

Women Pray: Voices through the Ages, from Many Faiths, Cultures and Traditions
Edited and with Introductions by Monica Furlong

5 x 7¼, 256 pp, Quality PB, 978-1-59473-071-9 **$15.99**
Deluxe HC with ribbon marker, 978-1-893361-25-6 **$19.95**

About SKYLIGHT PATHS Publishing

SkyLight Paths Publishing is creating a place where people of different spiritual traditions come together for challenge and inspiration, a place where we can help each other understand the mystery that lies at the heart of our existence.

Through spirituality, our religious beliefs are increasingly becoming a part of our lives—rather than *apart* from our lives. While many of us may be more interested than ever in spiritual growth, we may be less firmly planted in traditional religion. Yet, we do want to deepen our relationship to the sacred, to learn from our own as well as from other faith traditions, and to practice in new ways.

SkyLight Paths sees both believers and seekers as a community that increasingly transcends traditional boundaries of religion and denomination—people wanting to learn from each other, *walking together, finding the way.*

For your information and convenience, at the back of this book we have provided a list of other SkyLight Paths books you might find interesting and useful. They cover the following subjects:

Buddhism / Zen	Gnosticism	Mysticism
Catholicism	Hinduism /	Poetry
Children's Books	Vedanta	Prayer
Christianity	Inspiration	Religious Etiquette
Comparative	Islam / Sufism	Retirement
Religion	Judaism / Kabbalah /	Spiritual Biography
Current Events	Enneagram	Spiritual Direction
Earth-Based	Meditation	Spirituality
Spirituality	Midrash Fiction	Women's Interest
Global Spiritual	Monasticism	Worship
Perspectives		

Or phone, fax, mail or e-mail to: SKYLIGHT PATHS Publishing
Sunset Farm Offices, Route 4 • P.O. Box 237 • Woodstock, Vermont 05091
Tel: (802) 457-4000 • Fax: (802) 457-4004 • www.skylightpaths.com
Credit card orders: (800) 962-4544 (8:30AM–5:30PM ET Monday–Friday)
Generous discounts on quantity orders. SATISFACTION GUARANTEED. Prices subject to change.